Fisk's Funeral Procession passing his Grand Opera House.

COL. JAMES FISK, JR.

THE LIFE OF
Col. JAMES FISK, Jr.
"THE PRINCE OF ERIE."

—OF—

MISS HELEN JOSEPHINE MANSFIELD,
"THE ERIE PRINCESS."

—OF—

EDWARD L. STOKES,
THE ASSASSIN,

AND OF

HON. WM. M. TWEED,

Of New York, the Notorious Leader of the Infamous Tammany Ring.

—ALSO—

An Account of the Destruction of that Ring, and the Defeat of its Champions by Committee of 70.

Together with a Sketch of **The GRAND DUKE ALEXIS, of Russia,** his Home and Family.

ILLUSTRATED.

Published by J. W. GOODSPEED, Chicago, St. Louis, Cincinnati, and New Orleans.

H. S. GOODSPEED & CO., 37 Park Row, New York.

1872.

Entered according to Act of Congress, in the year 1872, by
J. W. GOODSPEED,
In the office of the Librarian of Congress, at Washington.

STEAM PRESS OF
OTTAWAY, BROWN & COLBERT,
7 & 9 South Jefferson St., Chicago.

A. ZEESE & CO.,
ELECTROTYPHERS,
Chicago.

THE LIFE

OF

JAMES FISK, Jr.

———o———

CHAPTER I.

HIS BIRTHPLACE—HIS BOYHOOD—HIS SCHOOLDAYS—HIS FIRST BUSINESS ENTERPRISE AS A FOOT PEDDLER—TRAVELS WITH VAN AMBURG—FORMS A PARTNERSHIP IN BOSTON—COTTON SPECULATIONS—GOVERNMENT SPECULATIONS, ETC., ETC.

Aptly, yet inaptly, it has been said of the Americans, that they are a sensational people—that we have sensation in every form in which it can be dished up to suit the varied tastes of the millions—sensation in prose and poem—sensation in sermon and drama, and that our thirst for it is insatiate, following us to the deathbed and to the grave—and alas, that, if the holy rest of heaven is unbroken by thrilling and sensational episodes, we shall soon weary of its quiet, and complain of its monotony. Be this as it may, and, perhaps, it had better pass unquestioned; it is not our purpose to cultivate what must be an evil. The lives of very many of those whose brief day passed as " a tale that is told," may well be compared to a pebble that is dropped into the bosom of the Ocean. For a moment tiny waves circle around it, then rest as if for ages they had lain unruffled. Once in a century or so, some being seems marked by the fates or the furies who preside over his birth, to sweep before us like a bright meteor across the sky, then go out in the immeasurable darkness and is forgotten, or like the withering breath of the hot simoon, leaving desolation in its track which years can scarce erase. It is to this class that the man who is the subject of the world's short lived wonder belongs, and we are grieved that the truthful historian can find so little of good in a life that might have been so grand a thing, with which to offset its many errors. More than thirty-seven years ago, in a quiet town that nestles amongst the green mountains whose verdant crown had given to the state the name it bears, it was said to the Father of the future "Prince of Erie," "to you a Son is born," and we will suppose that the mother in the fullness of her wifely joy and love, looked at her first born in his spotless innocence and said, "he shall be called *James*." Through the host of ills that baby flesh is heir to, no doubt he passed safely, and of "hair breadth 'scapes," and perils of every sort to which he was exposed we have no account until we hear of him as a rollicing, wild, good natured, wide awake schoolboy at Bratlesboro, who gave promise by his shrewd speculations in marbles, tops, knives, and strings, upon which boys of ten or twelve are wont to set their youthful affections, until such time as they are rivaled and eclipsed by loves of a very different sort; of that far seeing judgement which was to make him so successful in the business transactions of later life. His Father carried on, in a small way, a store and cotton factory, and his entire fortune would have been insufficient to cover the expense of one of those extravagant Bac-chinalian suppers that it was the pride and boast of the late James Fisk, jr., excelled anything of the kind given even in New York, whose dissipation and reckless expenditures shame ancient Babylon in her palmy days. At seventeen years of age we are informed that he took the position of clerk for his father, and thus became associated with him in business; but to rub from this part of his life, the little of gloss or varnish with which this might adorn it, and state facts in plain words he took charge of one of the peddling carts with which they transported their wares to the rural districts, where they were disposed of. He was a clever peddler, of dry goods, disposing of large quantities, and showing rare ingenuity at driving a close bargain, of which he invariably had the best side. Little by little the latent power which was in him developed, and dreams of a broader sphere of action, with the world for his field, and the corporate bodies that held wealth and power for his puppets to whom his word and will should be a law as imperative as any monarchs, filled his brain. Like the first and third Napoleons, he was a firm believer in destiny, and the vision of success was the one bright star upon which his eye was fixed, and standing at the wheel with his hand on the helm and his eye on that star, he guided by his self centered power, and indomitable will and energy, his ship with its precious treasure—freight safe over shoals and quicksand, and sunken rock, while the wreck of many a brave barque that sailed over smoother seas and through safer chanels, were tossed at the mercy of the waves around him. His nature strikes us as a compound of contradictions, selfish and avaricious, generous and liberal, defrauding deliberately and with malice aforethought, yet giving with a prodigal freeness, if but the impulse of the moment dictated it. The sufferers by the Chicago fires, will testify to the latter, while many an eastern man who sits, helpless, in almost beggary, will bear as strong witness to the former. Far back in his early life, while his ambition and his curiosity to see something of the world of men and things far exceeding his means to gratify it, he joined the traveling company of the somewhat celebrated Van Amburg, to quote one of the journals, "in the more than humble position of caretaker, whose highest occupation was to erect the tents, feed the animals, and clean their cages." However, if virtue is not without its own reward, neither is ability without recognition, and in due time the young man was advanced to the somewhat more respectable position of ticket seller, and as such, traveled with his employer eight years. The best sources from which we glean any authentic information of this part of his life, differ very materially in their statements, but certain it is that he returned to his old home, a wiser, though perhaps *not* a better man, and again engaged in business with his father. His policy then was worthy of his imitation in later years, though it seems to have been forgotten by him. His position as traveling salesman brought him in contact with every class of people, and he became very widely known. Their trade was extended through New England and western New York, and it is a somewhat significant fact that he was a general favorite among the ladies with whom he dealt, and that everywhere the advent of the future king of financiers was hailed with pleasure by the dames and lassies of both town and country. With a view to future operations, his plan was to furnish goods of a superior quality, at a profit which would but just insure him from loss, thus laying a broad and firm foundation for future business which would be both safe and honorable, and the name of the Fisks, father and son, were widely and favorably known as upright and honorable merchants, and no shadow of the disgrace that stains it now, rested upon it. The Boston wholesale house of Messrs. Jordon, Morse & Co., seeing in the young man those traits of character which would make him a desirable assistant, secured his services as salesman at their counters, but it was not long before he was admitted to the junior membership of the firm. The measure proved highly advantageous to both parties, though unquestionably more so for him than for them, since it placed him, for the first time in his life, in a position where he not only held the cards in his own hand to shuffle and cut, but to control the game and those who played against him, and Fisk, jr., would have been Fisk, jr., no longer had he neglected or overlooked this opportunity. Very much has been said by those who criticise his life, and who presume that they are fair judges of human nature, about his business talents, and his clear insight into the future, which seemed almost prophetic. At the risk of being considered egotistical and conceited, I must beg leave to differ from them. His ambition was boundless, but it was not honorable—he must stand first, but was not scrupulous as to manner or means, and with an unconquerable desire for celebrity, he only succeeded in becoming notorious. What is frequently dignified by the term "energetic devotion to business" was but the gambler's feverish mania for play and its attendant excitement. It was not possible for him to long keep on in the even tenor of his way, in the slow-going, legitimate track of a wholesale house, and our country's extremity was his opportunity. At the time when southern treachery wrung from the heart of the nation the bitterest drops of woe and grief that were ever wept, when the wailings of Rachaels rang over every hill and through every valley of the land we love, as they mourned for their children and refused to be comforted because they were not, this man, whom fulsome admirers style "so generous," conceived the grand idea of heaping his coffers from the treasury of a government already overburdened with the expense and anxiety of a civil war. I know how, being successful in those frauds, the world indulgently smiles at what it tenderly calls a "shrewd business transaction." Few seem to understand that *the people are paying taxes* on the $8,000,000 or $10.000,000 which he swindled the government out of in this first "little business transaction," in the form of a heavy national debt, which it will be years, not until "ashes to ashes" has been pronounced over this generation, will they be able to free themselves from. It is said that this was the real foundation of his fortune—the first firm basis which he had ever stood firmly upon. Soon after this, he established trading posts through all the war desolated south, buying up cotton at such low figures as the destitution of the people compelled them to accept. At Memphis, Nashville, New Orleans, and at every southern city where there were union soldiers in sufficient numbers to warrant the safety of his agents and his property, his daring ventures were rewarded with a golden harvest. At this late date, when the pain and sorrow of the Northern people has been softened by time and by experience, and when the abundant prosperity with which God has blessed us has placed us in a position where we can afford to be generous, and especially when we stand by the side of his new made grave, and his soul is in the hands of his Judge, it ill becomes us to heap upon the head of this man the epithets he has richly deserved. That he is no worse than thousands of other men who, living under the protection of the stripes and stars, were yet cowardly enough to wrap the Bonnie folds of the flag we venerate over their treasonable perfidy to the government, seems only to add to the sum of his actual guilt. In 1863 he visited New York with the view of employing, in a larger way, the money which he had acquired in the cotton business. It is not to be supposed that small gaines and slow profits would satisfy this man who dabbled in millions, and casting his eyes about for a fresh victim, and also for something whose tameness would not weary him, amused himself with the fancy that perhaps he might do well in the line of navigation, and accordingly he purchased the old Stonington line of steamers, consisting the Commodore, the Plymouth, and the Commonwealth, of the well-known Daniel Drew, for the sum of $750,000. The result of this was the formation of the company known as the Bristol line with a capital of $1,500,000. The ostensible object was to make money—the real object to bring his name before the public in as prominent a manner as possible, and at the same time to be in a position to safely gratify an old grudge against the Fall River line, in opposition to which his own ran.

Once on the threshold of prosperity, it needed but few bold strokes to carry him over. There is no doubt but the life of Fisk, jr., is one of the most rapidly-culminating and brilliantly-infamous to be found in the annuals of society. Ten years ago, Fisk was a sharp Yankee peddler, driving in his cart from place to place. Four years ago, he was merely a Wall-street broker, with a keen eye working on a moderate scale. A year later, he was at the head of a gigantic corporation, and able, by an hour's effort, to summon forces which should, at one swoop, gather into his clutches a score of millions of other people's property, impoverish a thousand wealthy men, or derange the values and the traffic of a vast empire. And to-day he is an unmourned victim of his own lewd and unscrupulous ways, while his accumulations of wealth and power are dissolving away ten times more rapidly than they were amassed.

Fisk's operation in connection with the Erie Railway, and cognate schemes, are too many to be referred to in any complete detail. They commenced, on such a scale as to become generally notorious, in the early part of 1868, when Daniel Drew, Cornelius Vanderbilt, and Eldridge, of the Boston, Hartford & Erie Railroad, settled their long and violent quarrel for the control of the Erie Railway, and divided the spoils among themselves. The Erie frauds had been set going nearly two years earlier, when Drew, to checkmate Vanderbilt's attempt to secure a majority of the Erie stock, made an over-issue of 60,000 shares. Vanderbilt met this by continuing to buy up the stock of the company, overissues and all, and by bringing all sorts of legal batteries to bear upon his antagonist. Drew retaliated in kind, and a long series of injunctions, decrees, orders of courts, and counter-orders ensued, which ended, as above mentioned, in a truce; Drew, Vanderbilt, and Eldridge dividing among them the proceeds of the various over-issues (for they had been kept up until the honest stockholders of the company had been robbed of more than half the value of their property), and awarding to Fisk and Gould the possession and management of the Erie Road, along with the shares remaining in the possession of the Ring. With this conveyance, Fisk and Gould obtained the implied power to squeeze the orange for what the residue of it was worth.

This combination of Fisk and Gould has since become so notorious that their name is now accepted as the synonym for all that is dark and deceitful; but it would appear that they then were much less versed in chicanery than the older knaves whose loot they shared on this occasion. At least Fisk claims to have been, at that time, a very proper young man. This transaction, by which he and his partner were made in some sense the scapegoats, and in some sense the legatees, of Drew, Vanderbilt, and Eldridge, is thus described by Fisk himself, in a statement made from the witness stand during the trial of one of the many suits in which the concern subsequently became involved:

Finally, (says Fisk), about 12 o'clock a paper was passed round and we signed it; I don't know what it contained; I didn't read it; I don't think I noticed a word of it; I remember the space for the names was greater than that covered by the writing; my impression is that I took my hat and left at once in disgust; I told Gould we had sold ourselves to the devil; I presume that was not the only document signed; I remember seeing Mr. White, the cashier, come in with the check-book, and I said to him, "You are bearing in the remains of this corporation to be put in Vanderbilt's tomb." No; I didn't know the contents of the paper which I signed, and I have always been glad that I didn't; I have thought of it a thousand times; I don't know what other documents I signed; I signed everything that was put before me; after once the devil had hold of me I kept on signing; didn't read any of them, and have no idea what they were; I don't know how many I signed; I kept no count after the first one; I went with the robbers then, and I have been with them ever since; my impression is, that after the signing I left at once; I don't know whether we sat down or not; we didn't have anything to eat, I know.

Having once, as he says, joined the band of robbers, Fisk became, like many another neophyte, the most zealous of all; and, combining his own unlimited assurance with Gould's decided talent for intrigue, he had soon added largely to the illegal over-issues of stock, and sent the price down below 25, whereas it had been near to par before the rascals got possession of it. The actual effects of the Erie Road had probably been thrown to Fisk and Gould as a rather undesirable possession, of which the older rogues were glad to be rid; but the new managers proved more cunning than their owlish predecessors. Taking in Tweed and Sweeny as directors, they of course got Barnard and Cardozo, the Tammany judges, among the assets contributed by that pair of worthies; and it was not long before they had squeezed a full million out of Drew, and enlarged their scale of operations to an amazing extent. Among the most brilliant strokes of the Gould genius was the act by which the Albany legislature legalized their past over-issues, and the Classification Act, by which they and their creatures were continued in the directory for six years, the stockholders being rendered entirely helpless by the act.

In the summer of 1869, occurred the raid upon the Albany and Susquehanna railroad, by which that road was seized;—the act being a most flagrant robbery. The adjuncts to this nefarious operation were orders and injunctions *ad libitum* from Barnard; a packing of a shareholders' meeting with shoulder-hitters bearing bogus proxies;

and, finally, a military seizure of the road, in defiance of law and right, from which they were only ousted by the state militia.

Almost simultaneously with the Albany and Susquehanna campaign (the theft of the English shares occurred previously), came the great Gold Conspiracy, which culminated in September, 1869, and of which Fisk and Gould were the controlling spirits. Of this affair it must be said that there was nothing unlawful in it, although it involved a complete derangement of trade, and, probably, the financial ruin of thousands of men, all through the country, who were not voluntary or directly connected with the affair. It also involved tampering with the national treasury; and, to accomplish this, the chief magistrate of the nation was approached—unsuccessfully, however—by such considerations, and through such channels, as the conspirators deemed most practicable. They failed; and when Fisk, as a consequence, repudiated his contracts, he was forced to flee for his life, and lock himself up in his strong castle, the Grand Opera House.

The edifice referred to is one of the monuments of Fisk's love of display and of personal notoriety. Into the *operas bouffe*, the spectacles, the military regiments, the Long Branch parades, the steamboats, the brass bands, and the long array of bedizened harlots whom he supported, went the earnings of the Erie road, and Fisk's share of the profits which Gould's cunning conjured out of the firm's transactions. The foibles of the shrewd Yankee pedler in this direction brought upon him his sudden and violent end, just as the iniquity of his more weighty operations in the field of finance were about to bring upon his worthless head their own disastrous consequences

CHAPTER II.

STARTS IN LIFE AS A PEDDLER—BECOMES PARTNER IN A BOSTON HOUSE—BUSINESS RELATIONS WITH DANIEL DREW—DESCRIPTION OF HIS PERSONAL APPEARANCE—OF GOULD'S—HIS OPINION OF HIS FATHER'S HONESTY—INTRIGUES WITH THE BOARD OF DIRECTORS—HE BUYS THE OPERA HOUSE.

Perhaps nothing could be more appropos just here, than the racy and satirical articles from the pen of Charles F. and Henry Adams.

He came originally from Vermont, probably the most respectable and correct State in the Union, and his father had been a peddler who sold goods from town to town in his native valley of the Connecticut. The son followed his father's calling with boldness and success. He drove his huge wagon, made resplendent with paint and varnish, with four or six horses, through the towns of Vermont and Western Massachusetts; and when his father remonstrated in alarm at his reckless management, the young man, with his usual bravado, took his father into his service, at a fixed salary, with a warning that he was not to put on airs on the strength of his new dignity. A large Boston firm which had supplied his goods on credit, attracted by his energy, took him into the house; the war broke out; his influence drew the firm into some bold speculations which were successful; in a few years he retired with some $20,000, which he subsequently lost. He formed a connection with Daniel Drew in New York, and a new sign, ominous of future trouble, was raised in Wall street, bearing the names of Fisk & Belden, brokers.

Personally Mr. Fisk was coarse, noisy, boastful, ignorant; the type of a young butcher in appearance and mind. Nothing could be more striking than the contrast between him and his future associate, Gould. One was small and slight in person, sallow, reticent and stealthy, with a trace of Jewish origin. The other was large, florid, gross, talkative, and obstreperous. Mr. Fisk's redeeming point was his humor, which had a strong flavor of American nationality. His mind was extraordinary fertile in ideas and expedients, while his conversation was filled with unusual images and strange forms of speech, which were caught up and made popular by the New York press. In respect to honesty as between Gould and Fisk, the latter was, perhaps, if possible, less deserving of trust than the former. A story not without a keen stroke of satirical wit, is told by him, which illustrates his estimate of abstract truth. An old woman who had bought of the older Fisk a handkerchief which cost ninepence in the New England currency, where six shillings are reckoned to the dollar, complained to Mr. Fisk, Jr., that his father had cheated her. Mr. Fisk considered the case maturely, and gave a decision based on *a priori* principles. "No," said he, "the old man wouldn't have told you a lie for ninepence;" and then, as if this assertion needed some reasonable qualification, he added, "though he would have told eight of them for a dollar!" This destinction as regards the father may have been just, since the father seems to have held old-fashioned ideas as to wholesale and retail-trade; but in regard to the son even this relative degree of truth cannot be predicted with any truth, since, if the Investigating Committee of Congress and its evidence are to be believed, Mr. Fisk seldom or never speaks truth at all.

An intrigue equally sucessful and disreputable brought these two men into the Erie Board of Directors, whence they speedily drove their more timid predecessor, Drew. In July, 1868, Gould made himself President and Treasurer of the corporation. Fisk became Comptroller. A young lawyer, named Lane, became counsel. These three Directors made a majority of the Executive Committee, and were masters of Erie. The Board of Directors held no meetings. The Executive Committee was never called together, and the three men—Fisk, Gould, and Lane—became from this time the absolute, irresponsible owners of the Erie Railway, not less than if it had been their personal property and plaything.

This property was in effect, like all the great railway corporations, an empire within a republic. It consisted of a trunk line of road 459 miles in length, with branches 314 miles in extent, or 773 miles of road in all. Its capital stock amounted to £7,000,000. Its gross receipts exceeded £3,000,000 per annum. It employed not less than 15,000 men, and supported their families. Over all this wealth and influence, greater than that directly swayed by any private citizen, greater than is absolutely and personally controlled by most kings, and far too great for the public safety, either in a democracy, or in any other form of society, the vicissitudes of a troubled time placed two men in irresponsible authority; and both these men belonged to a low and degraded moral and social type. Such an elevation has been rarely seen in modern history. Even the most dramatic of modern authors, even Balzac himself, who so loved to deal with similar violent alternations of fortune, or Alexander Dumas, with all his extravagance of imagination, never have reached a conception bolder or more melodramatic than this, nor have they ever ventured to conceive a plot so enormous, or a catastrophe so original, as was now to be developed.

One of the earliest acts of the new rulers was such as Balzac or Dumas might have predicted and delighted in. They established themselves in a palace. The old offices of the Erie railway were in the lower part of the city, among the wharves and warehouses a situation, no doubt, convenient for business, but by no means agreeable as a residence; and the new proprietors naturally wished to reside on their property. Mr. Fisk and Mr. Gould accordingly bought a huge building of white marble, not unlike a European palace, situated about two miles from the business quarter, and containing a large theatre or opera house. They also purchased several smaller houses adjoining it. The opera house cost about $140,000, and a large part of the building was at once leased, by the two purchasers, to themselves as the Erie corporation, to serve as offices. This suite of apartments was then furnished by themselves, as representing the corporation, at an expense of some $60,000, and in a style which, though called vulgar, is certainly not more vulgar than that of the persident's official residence, and which would be magnificent in almost any palace in Europe. The adjoining houses were connected with the main building; and in one of these Mr. Fisk had his private apartments, with a private passage to his opera-box. He also assumed direction of the theatre, of which he became manager-in-chief. To these royal arrangements he brought tastes which have been commonly charged as the worst results of royal license. The atmosphere of the Erie offices was not supposed to be disturbed with moral prejudices; and as the opera itself supplied Mr. Fisk's mind with amusements, so the opera *troupe* supplied him with a permanent harem. Whatever Mr. Fisk did was on an extraordinary scale.

HOW FISK AND GOULD GOT POSSESSION OF THE ERIE RAILWAY.

Daniel Drew and his then lieutenants, James Fisk, jr., and Jay

Gould, had fled to Jersey City, in the summer of 1868, to avoid arrest by Judge Barnard, in an action commenced against them by Cornelius Vanderbilt, for an over issue of 60,000 shares of Erie stock in defiance of Barnard's injunction.

Early in April, Mr. Drew took advantage of that blessed immunity from arrest which the Sabbath confers on the hunted of the law, to revisit the familiar scenes across the river. His visit soon resulted in conferences between himself and Vanderbilt, and these conferences naturally led to overtures of peace. Though the tide was turning against the great railroad king, though an uncontrollable popular feeling was fast bearing down his schemes of monopoly, yet he was by no means beaten or subdued. His plans, however, had evidently failed for the present; as he expressed himself, he could easily enough buy the Erie railway, but he could not buy up the printing-press. It was clearly his interest to abandon his late line of attack, and to bide his time patiently, or to possess himself of his prey by some other method. The wishes of all parties, therefore, were fixed on a settlement, and no one was disposed to stand out except in order to obtain better terms. The interests, however, were multifarious. There were four parties to be taken care of, and the depleted treasury of the Erie railway was doomed to suffer.

The details of this masterpiece of Wall street diplomacy have never come to light, but Mr. Drew's visits to New York became more frequent and less guarded; by the middle of April he had appeared in Broad street on a week-day, undisturbed by fears of arrest, and soon rumors began to spread of misunderstandings between himself and his brother exiles. It was said that his continual absences alarmed them; that they distrusted him; that his terms of settlement were not theirs. It was even asserted that his orders on the treasury were no longer honored, and that he had, in fact, ceased to be a power in Erie. Whatever truth there may have been in these rumors, it was very evident his associates had no inclination to trust themselves within the reach of the New York courts until a definite treaty, satisfactory to themselves, was signed and sealed. This probably took place about the 25th of April; for on that day the Erie camp at "Fort Taylor," as their uninviting hotel had been dubbed, was broken up, the president and one of the executive committee took steamer for Boston, and the other directors appeared before Judge Barnard, prepared to purge themselves of their contempt.

Though the details of negotiation have never been divulged, yet it was clear enough what three of the four parties desired. Commodore Vanderbilt wished to be relieved of the vast amount of stock with which he was loaded, and his friends, Work and Shell, in whose names the battle had been fought, must be protected. Mr. Drew desired to settle his entangled accounts as treasurer, and to obtain a release in full, which might be pleaded in future complications. Mr. Eldridge and his Boston friends were sufficiently anxious to be relieved of the elephant they found on their hands, in the Erie Railway of New York, and to be at leisure to devote the spoils of their victim to the development of their New England enterprise. Messrs. Gould and Fisk alone were unprovided for, and they alone presented themselves as obstacles to be overcome by railroad diplomacy.

CHAPTER III.

PEACE ANNOUNCED TO THE BOARD—TERMS AGREED UPON BETWEEN THE PARTIES—WORK AND SCHELL PAID OFF—DREW LEFT IN PEACE AND PLENTY—GOULD AND FISK IN UNDISPUTED CONTROL—LEGAL COMPLICATIONS—FEAR AND TREMBLING—DESPERATE SHIFTS—BRITISH POLICY—FIRST APPEARANCE OF TWEED AND SWEENY.

At last, upon the 2d of July, Mr. Eldridge formally announced to the Board of Directors that the terms of peace had been agreed upon. Commodore Vanderbilt was, in the first place, provided for. He was to be relieved of 50,000 shares of Erie stock at 70, receiving therefor $2,500,000 in cash, and $1,250,000 in bonds of the Boston, Hartford & Erie, at 80. He was also to receive a further sum of $1,000,000 outright, as a consideration for the privilege the Erie Road thus purchased, of calling upyn him for his remaining 50,000 shares at 70 at any time within four months. He was also to have two seats in the Board of Directors, and all suits were to be dismissed and offences condoned. The sum of $429,250 was fixed upon as a proper amount to assuage the sense of wrong from which his two friends, Work and Shell, had suffered, and to efface from their memories all recollection of the unfortunate "pool" of the previous December. Why the owners of the Erie Railway should have paid this indemnity of $4,000,000 is not very clear. The operations were apparently outside of the business of a railway company, and no more connected with the stockholders of the Erie than were the butchers' bills of the individual doctors.

While Vanderbilt, and his friends, were thus provided for, Mr. Drew was to be left in undisturbed enjoyment of the fruits of his recent operations, but was to pay into the treasury $540,000 and interest, in full discharge of all claims and causes of action which the Erie Company might have against him. The Boston party, as represented by Mr. Eldridge, was to be relieved of $5,000,000 of the Boston,

Hartford & Erie bonds, for which they were to receive $4,000,000 of Erie acceptances. None of these parties, therefore, had anything to complain of, whatever might have been the sensations of the real owners of the railway. A total amount of some $9,000,000 in cash was drawn from the treasury in fulfilment of this *settlement*, as the persons concerned were pleased to term this remarkable disposition of property entrusted to their care.

Messrs. Gould and Fisk still remained to be taken care of, and to them their associates left—*the Erie Railway.* * * * *

WHAT THEY DID WITH IT.

Thus, in the early days of July, 1868, Messrs. Fisk and Gould found themselves beginning life, as it were, in absolute control of the Erie Railway, but with an empty treasury and a doubtful reputation. Outwardly, things did not look unpromising. The legal complications were settled, and the fearful load imposed by the settlement upon the already overburdened resources of the road was not, of course, imparted to the public. It is unnecessary to add that the "outside" holders of the stock were, in the counsels of the managers, included in the public inquiries which, in regard to the affairs of the company were looked upon by the ring in control as downright impertinence. A calm—deceitful indeed, but yet a calm—succeeded the severe agitations of the money market. All through the month of July money was easy and ruled at 3 or 4 per cent; Erie was consequently high, and was quoted at about 70, which enabled the company to dispose without the Vanderbilt stock. It may well be believed that Messrs. Fisk and Gould could not have regarded their empty treasury, just depleted to the extent of nine millions—trust funds misapplied by Directors in the processes of stock-gambling—without serious question as to their ability to save the road from bankruptcy. The October election was approaching. Vanderbilt was still a threatening element in the future, and new combinations might arise. Millions were necessary, and must at once be forthcoming. The new officials were, however, men of resources, and were not men of many scruples. The money must be raised, and recent experience indicated a method of raising it. Their policy, freed from the influence of Drew's vascillating, treacherous, and withal timid nature, could now be bold and direct. The pretence of resistance to monopoly would always serve them, as it had served them before, as a plausible and popular cry. Above all, their councils were free from interlopers and spies; for the first act of Messrs. Gould and Fisk had been to do away with the old Board of Auditors, and to concentrate all power in their own hands as President, Treasurer, and Comptroller. Fortunately for them it was midsummer, and the receipts of the road were very heavy, supplying them with large sums of ready money; most fortunately for them also, a strange infatuation at this time took possession of the English mind.

Shrewd as the British capitalist proverbially is, his judgment in regard to American investments has been singularly fallible. When our national bonds went begging at a discount of 60 per cent, he transmitted them to Germany and refused to touch them himself. At the very same time a class of railroad securities—such as those of this very Erie Railway, or, to cite a yet stronger case, those of the Atlantic & Great Western Road—was gradually absorbed in London as an honest investment, long after these securities had "gone into the street" in America. It was this strange fatuity which did much to bring on the crash of May, 1866. Even that did not seem to teach wisdom to the British bankers, who had apparently passed from the extreme of caution to the extreme of confidence. They now, after all the exposures of the preceding months, rush into Erie, apparently because it seemed cheap, and the prices in New York were sustained by the steady demand for stock on foreign account. Not only did this curious infatuation, involving purchases to the extent of a hundred thousand shares, cover up the operations of the new ring, but, at a later period, the date of the possible return of this stock to Wall street, was the hinge on which the success of its culminating plot was made to turn.

The appearance of calm lasted but thirty days. Early in August it was evident that something was going on. Erie suddenly fell 10 per cent; in a few days more it experienced a further fall of 7 per cent, touching 44 by the 19th of the month, upon which day, to the astonishment of Wall street, the transfer-books of the company were closed preparatory to the annual election. As this election was not to take place until the 13th of October, and as the books had thus been closed thirty days in advance of the usual time, it looked very much as though the managers were satisfied with the present disposition of the stock, and meant, by keeping it where it was, to preclude any such unpleasantness as an opposition ticket. The courts and a renewed war of injunctions were of course open to any contestants, including Commodore Vanderbilt, who might desire to avail themselves of them; probably, however, the memory of recent struggles was too fresh to permit any one to embark on those treacherous waters. At any rate, nothing of the sort was attempted The election took place at the usual time, and the ring in control voted itself, without opposition, into a new lease of power. Two new names had meanwhile appeared in the list of Erie Directors,—those of Peter B. Sweeny and William M. Tweed, the two most prominent leaders of that notorious ring which controls the proletarriat of New York city and governs the politics of the State. The alliance was an ominous one, for the construction of the new Board can be stated in few words, and calls for no comment. It consisted of the Erie ring and the Tammany ring, brought together in close political and financial union; and, for the rest, a working majority of supple tools and a hopeless minority of respectable figureheads. This formidable combination shot out its feelers far and wide; it wielded the influence of a great corporation with a capital of $100,000,000; it controlled the politics of the first city of the New World; it sent its representatives to the Senate of the State, and numbered among its agents the Judges of the courts. Compact, disciplined, and reckless, it knew its own power and would not scruple to use it.

It was now the month of October, and the harvest had been gathered. The ring and its allies determined to reap their harvest also, and that harvest was to be nothing less than a contribution levied, not only upon Wall street and New York, but upon all the immense interests, commercial and financial, which radiate from New York all over the country. Like the Cæsar of old, they issued their edict that all the world should be taxed. The process was not novel, but it was effective. A momentary stringency may be looked for in New York at certain seasons of every year. It is generally most severe in the autumn months, when the crops have to be moved, and the currency is drained steadily away from the financial centre toward the extremities of the system. The method by which an artificial stringency is produced is thus explained in a recent report of the comptroller of the currency : " It is scarcely possible to avoid the inference that nearly one-half of the available resources of the national banks in the city of New York are used in the operations of the Stock and Gold Exchange ; that they are loaned upon the security of stocks which are bought and sold largely on speculation, and which are manipulated by cliques and combinations, according as the bulls or bears are for the moment in the ascendancy. * * * Taking advantage of an active demand for money to move the crops west and south, shrewd operators form their combinations to depress the market by " locking up " money,— withdrawing all they can control or borrow from the common fund; money becomes scarce; the rate of interest advances, and stocks decline. The legitimate demand for money continues; and, fearful of trenching on their reserve, the banks are strained for means. They dare not call in their demand loans, for that would compel their customers to sell securities on a falling market, which would make matters worse. Habitually lending their means to the utmost limit of prudence, and their credit much beyond that limit, to brokers and speculators, they are powerless to afford relief; their customers, by the force of circumstances, become their masters. The banks cannot hold back or withdraw from the dilemma in which their mode of doing business has placed them. They must carry the load to save their margins. A panic which should greatly reduce the price of securities, would occasion serious, if not fatal, results to the banks most extensively engaged in such operations, and would produce a feeling of insecurity which would be very dangerous to the entire banking interests of the country."

FISK'S HORSE AND GROOM.

CHAPTER IV.

OVER ISSUES OF ERIE STOCK—INVESTIGATION—"CERTAIN CONTINGENCIES"—NEW ISSUES STILL FORCED FORWARD—DECISION REGARDING THE RECEIVERSHIP—GREAT GOLD CONSPIRACY.

All this machinery was now put in motion; the banks and their customers were forced into the false position described, and toward the end of October it had become perfectly notorious in Wall street that large new issues of Erie had been made, and that these new issues were intimately connected with the sharp stringency then existing in the money market. It was at last determined to investigate the matter, and upon the 27th of the month a committee of three was appointed by the Stock Exchange to wait upon the officers of the corporation with the view of procuring such information as they might be willing to impart. The committee called on Mr. Gould and stated the object of their visit. In reply to their inquiries Mr. Gould informed them that Erie convertible bonds for ten millions of dollars had been issued, half of which had already been, and the rest of which would be, converted into stock; that the money had been devoted to the purchase of Boston, Hartford and Erie bonds for five millions, and also, of course, to payments for steel rails. The committee desired to know if any further issue of stock was in contemplation, but were obliged to rest satisfied with a calm assurance that no new issue was just then contemplated except "in certain contingencies;" from which enigmatical utterances Wall street was left to infer that the exigencies of Messrs. Gould & Fisk were elements not to be omitted from any calculations as to the future of Erie and the money market. The amount of these issues of new stock was, of course, soon whispered in a general way; but it was not till months afterward that a sworn statement of the secretary of the Erie railway revealed the fact that the stock of the corporation had been increased from $34,265,300 on the 1st of July, 1868. the date when Drew and his associates had left it, to $57,-766,300 on the 24th of October of the same year, or by 235,000 shares in four months. This, too, had been done without consultation with the board of directors, and with no other authority than that conferred by the ambiguous resolution of February 19. Under that resolution the stock of the company had now been increased 138 per cent in eight months. Such a process of inflation may, perhaps, be justly considered the most extraordinary feat of financial legerdemain which history has yet recorded.

Now, however, when the committee of the Stock Exchange had returned to those who sent them, the mask was thrown off, and operations were conducted with vigor and determination. New issues of Erie were continually forced upon the market untll the stock fell to 35 ; greenbacks were locked up in the vaults of the banks, until the unexampled sum of twelve millions was withdrawn from circulation; the prices of securities and merchandise declined; trade and the autumnal movement of the crops were brought almost to a standstill; and loans became more and more difficult to negotiate, until at lenght even 1 1-2 per cent a day was paid for carrying stocks. Behind all this it was notorious that some one was pulling the wires, the slightest touch upon which sent a quiver through every nerve of the great financial organism, and wrung private gain from public agnoy. The strange proceeding reminds one of those scenes in the chambers of Inquisition, where the judges calmly put their victim to the question, until his spasms warned them not to exceed the limits of human indurance. At last the public distress reached the ears of the Government at Washington. While it was simply the gamblers of Wall street who were tearing each other, their clamor for relief excited little sympathy. When, however, the suffering had extended through all the legitimate business circles of the country,—when the scarcity of money threatened to cut off the winter food of the poor, to rob the farmer of the fruits of his toil, and to bring ruin upon half the debtor class of the community,—then even Mr. McCulloch, pledged as he was to contraction, was moved to interfere. The very revenues of the Government were affected by the operation of gamblers. They were therefore informed that, if necessary, fifty millions of additional currency would be forthcoming to the relief of the community, and then, and not till then, the screws were loosened.

THE ERIE DIRECTOR'S BILL.

It was not until the 10th of February that Judge Cardozo published his decision setting aside the Sutherland Receivership, and establishing on a basis of authority the right to over-issue stock at pleasure. The subject was then as obsolete and forgotten as though it had never absorbed the public attention. And another "settlement" had already been effected. The details of this arrangement have not been dragged to light through the exposures of subsequent litigation. But it is not difficult to see where and how a combination of overpowering influence may have been effected, and a guess might even be hazarded as to its objects and its victims. The fact that a settlement had been arrived at was intimated in the papers of the 26th of December. On the 19th of the same month a stock dividend of 80 per cent. in the New York Central had been suddenly declared by Vanderbilt. Presently the Legislature met. While the Erie Ring seemed to have good reasons for apprehending hostile legislation, Vanderbilt, on his part, might have feared for the success of a bill which was to legalize his new stock. But hardly a voice was raised against the Erie men, and the bill of the Central was safely carried through. This curious absence of opposition did not stop here, and soon the two parties were seen united in an active alliance. Vanderbilt wanted to consolidate his roads; the Erie Directors wanted to avoid the formality of annual elections. Thereupon two other bills went hastily through this honest and patriotic Legislature, the one authorizing the Erie Board, which had been elected for one year, to classify itself so that one fifth only of its members should vacate office during each succeeding year, the other consolidating the Vanderbilt roads into one colossal monopoly. Public interests and private rights seem equally to have been the victims. It is impossible to say that the beautiful unity of interests which led to such results was the fulfilment of the December settlement; but it is a curious fact that the same paper which announced in one column that Vanderbilt's two measures, known as the consolidation and Central scrip bills had gone to the Governor for signature, should, in another, have reported the discontinuance of the Belmont and Whelpley suits by the consent of all interested. It may be that public and private interests were not thus balanced and traded away in a servile Legislature, but the strong probabilities are that the settlement of December made white even that of July. Meanwhile, the conquerors,—the men whose names had been made notorious through the whole land in all these infamous proceedings,—were at last undisputed masters of the situation, and no man questioned the firmness of their grasp on the Erie Railway. They walked erect and proud of their infamy through the streets of our great cities; they voluntarily subjected themselves to that to which other depredators are compelled to submit, and, by exposing their portraits in public conveyance, converted noble steamers into branch galleries of a police office.

THE GREAT GOLD CONSPIRACY.

The great gold conspiracy of September, 1869, was a conception of Mr. Jay Gould's. Fisk does not appear in it until Corbin, President Grant's brother-in-law, and Butterfield, the assistant treasurer of the United States at New York, had been relieved.

Down to this moment, Mr. James Fisk, jr., has not appeared in the affair. Gould had not taken him into his confidence; and it was not until after the 10th of September that Gould appears to have decided that there was nothing else to be done. Fisk was not a safe ally in so delicate an affair, but apparently there was no choice. Gould approached him; and, as usual, his touch was like magic. Mr. Fisk's evidence begins here, and may be believed when very strongly corroborated:

Gold having settled down to 35, and I not having cared to touch it, he was a little sensitive on the subject, feeling as if he would rather take his losses without saying anything about it. * * * One day he said to me, "Don't you think gold has got to the bottom?" I replied that I did not see the profit in buying gold unless you have got into a position where you can command the market. He then said he had bought quite a large amount of gold, and I judged from his conversation that he wanted me to go into the movement and help strengthen the market. Upon that I went into the market and bought. I should say that was about the 15th or 16th of September. I bought at that time about seven or eight millions, I think.

The market responded slowly to these enormous purchases; and on the 16th the clique was still struggling to recover its lost ground.

Meanwhile Mr. Gould had placed another million and a half of gold to the account of General Butterfield, and notified him of the purchase. So Mr. Gould swears in spite of General Butterfield's denial. The date of this purchase is not fixed. Through Mr. Corbin a notice was also sent by Gould, about the middle of September to the President's private Secretary, General Porter, informing him that half a million was placed to his credit. General Porter instantly wrote to repudiate the purchase, but it does not appear that Butterfield took any notice of Gould's transaction on his account. On the 10th of September the President had again come to New York, where he remained his brother-in-law's guest till the 13th; and during this visit Mr. Gould appears again to have seen him, although Mr. Corbin avers that on this occasion the President intimated his wish to the servant that this should be the last time Mr. Gould obtained admission. "Gould was always trying to get something out of him," he said; and if he had known how much Mr. Gould had succeeded in getting out of him, he would have admired the man's genius, even while shutting the door in his face. On the morning of the 13th the President set out on a journey to the little town of Washington, situated among the mountains of Western Pennsylvania, where he was to remain a few days. Mr. Gould, who now consulted Mr. Corbin regularly every morning and evening, was still extremely nervous in regard to the President's policy; and as the crisis approached, this nervousness led him into the fatal blunder of doing too much. The bribe offered to Porter was a grave mistake, but a greater mistake yet was made by pressing Mr. Corbin's influence too far. He induced Mr. Corbin to write an official article for the New York press on the financial policy of the government, an article afterwards inserted in the New York *Times* through the kind offices of Mr. James McHenry, and he also pursuaded or encouraged Mr. Corbin to write a letter directly to the President himself. This letter, written on the 17th, under the influence of Gould's anxiety, was instantly sent away by a special messenger of Fisk's to reach the President before he returned to the capital. The messenger carried also a letter of introduction to General Porter, the private Secretary, in order to secure the personal delivery of this important despatch.

We have now come to the week which was to witness the explosion of all this elaborately constructed mine. On Monday, the 20th, gold again rose. Throughout Tuesday and Wednesday Fisk continued to purchase without limit, and forced the price up to 40. At this time Gould's firm of Smith, Gould & Martin, through which the operation was conducted, had purchased some $50,000,000; and yet the bears went on selling, although they could only continue the contest by borrowing Gould's own gold. Gould, on the other hand, could no longer sell and clear himself, for the very reason that the sale of $50,000,000 would have broken the market to nothing. The struggle had become intense. The whole country was looking on with astonishment at the battle between the bulls and the bears. All business was deranged, and all values unsettled. There were indications of a panic in the stock market; and the bears in their emergency were vehemently pressing the Government to intervene. Gould now wrote to Mr. Boutwell a letter so inconceivably impudent that it indicates desperation and entire lose of his ordinary coolness. He began:

SIR: There is a panic in Wall street, engineered by a bear combination. They have withdrawn currency to such an extent that it is impossible to do ordinary business. The Erie company requires $800,000 to disburse. * * * Much of it in Ohio, where an exciting political contest is going on, and where we have about 10,000 employed, and the trouble is charged on the administration. * * * Cannot you, consistently, increase your line of currency?

From a friend such a letter would have been an outrage; but from a member of the Tammony Ring, the principal object of detestation to the government, such a threat or bribe—whichever it may be called was incredible. Mr. Gould was, in fact, at his wits' end. He dreaded a panic, and he felt it could no longer be avoided.

THE ATTEMPT TO ENTRAP PRESIDENT GRANT.

The scene now shifts for a moment to the distant town of Washington, among the hills of western Pennsylvania. On the morning of the 19th of September, President Grant and his private secretary, General Porter, were playing croquet on the grass, when Fisk's messenger, after twenty-four hours of travel by rail and carriage, arrived at the house, and sent in to ask for General Porter. When the president's game was ended, General Porter came, received his own letter from Corbin, and called the president, who entered the room and took his brother-in-law's despatch. He then left the room, and, after some ten or fifteen minutes' absence, returned. The messenger, tired of waiting, then asked, "Is it all right?" "All right," replied the president; and the messenger hastened to the nearest telegraph station and sent word to Fisk. "Delivered; all right."

HOW IT FAILED.

The messenger was, however, altogether mistaken. Not only was all not right, but all was going hopelessly wrong. The President, it appears, had at the outset supposed the man to be an ordinary Postoffice agent, and the letter an ordinary letter which had arrived through the Postoffice. Nor was it until Porter asked some curious question as to the man, that the President learned of his having been sent by Corbin merely to carry this apparently unimportant letter of advice. The President's suspicions were at once excited, and the same evening, at his request, Mrs. Grant wrote a hurried note to Mrs.

Corbin, telling her how greatly the President was distressed at the rumor that Mr. Corbin was speculating in Wall street, and how much he hoped that Mr. Corbin would "instantly disconnect himself with anything of that sort."

This letter, subsequently destroyed or said to have been destroyed by Mrs. Corbin, arrived in New York on the morning of Wednesday the 22d, the same day on which Gould and his enemies, the bears, were making their simultaneous appeals to Secretary Boutwell. Mrs. Corbin was greatly excited and distressed by her sister-in-law's language. She at once carried the letter to her husband, and insisted that he should instantly abandon his interest in the gold speculation. Mr. Corbin, although he considered the scruples of his wife and her family to be highly absurd, assented to her wish; and when Mr Gould came that evening as usual, with $50,000,000 of gold on his hands, and extreme anxiety on his mind, Corbin read to him two letters; the first, written by Mrs. Grant to Mrs. Corbin; the second, written by Mr. Corbin to President Grant, assuring him that he had not a dollar of interest in gold. The assurance of this second letter was, at any sacrifice, to be made good.

BLACK FRIDAY.

It was the morning of Thursday, the 3d; Gould and Fisk went to Broad street together, but, as usual, Gould was silent and secret, while Fisk was noisy and communicative. There was now a complete separation in their movements. Gould acted entirely through his own firm of Smith, Gould & Martin, while Fisk operated principally through his old partner Belden. One of Smith's principal brokers testifies:

"Fisk never could do business with Smith, Gould & Martin very comfortably. They would not do business for him. It was a very uncertain thing, of course, where Fisk might be. He is an erratic sort of genius. I don't think anybody would want to follow him very long. I am satisfied that Smith, Gould & Martin controlled their own gold, and were ready to do as they pleased with it without consulting Fisk. I do not think there was any general agreement.... None of us who knew him cared to do business with him. I would not have taken an order from him, nor had anything to do with him." Belden was considered a very low fellow. "I never had anything to do with him or his party," said one broker employed by Gould. "They were men I had a perfect detestation of; they were no company for me. I should not have spoken to them at all under any ordinary circumstances." Another says, " Belden is a man in whom I never had any confidence in any way. For months before that, I would not have taken him for a gold transaction."

And yet Belden bought millions upon millions of gold. He himself says he had bought twenty millions by this Thursday evening, and this without capital or credit except that of his brokers. Meanwhile Gould, on reaching the city, had at once given secret orders to sell. From the moment he left Corbin, he had but one idea, which was to get rid of his gold as quietly as possible. "I purchased merely enough to make believe I was a bull," says Gould. This double process continued all that afternoon. Fisk's wild purchases carried the price up to 144, and the panic in the street became more and more serious as the bears realized the extremity of their danger. No one can tell how much gold, which did not exist, they had contracted to deliver or pay the difference in price. One of the clique brokers swears that on this Thursday evening the street had sold the clique $118,000,000 of gold, and every rise of 1 per cent on this sum implied a loss of more than $200,000 to the bears. Naturally the terror was extreme, for half Broad street and thousands of speculators would have been ruined if compelled to settle gold at 105 which they had sold at 140.

When the next day came, Gould and Fisk went together to Broad street, and took possession of the private back office of a principal broker, "without asking the privilege of doing so," as the broker observes in his evidence. The first news brought to Gould was a disaster. The government had sent three men from Washington to examine the bank which Gould owned, and the bank sent word to Mr. Gould that it feared to certify for him as usual, and was itself in danger of a panic, caused by the presence of officers, which created distrust of the bank. It barely managed to save itself. Gould took the information silently, and his firm redoubled sales of gold. His partner, Smith, gave the orders to one broker after another, "Sell ten millions!" "The order was given as quick as a flash, and away he went," says one of these men. "I sold only eight millions." "Sell, sell, sell! do nothing but sell!—only don't sell to Fisk's brokers," were the orders which Smith himself acknowledges. In the Gold Room, Fisk's brokers were shouting their rising bids, and the packed crowd grew frantic with terror and rage as each successive rise showed their increasing losses. The wide streets outside were thronged with excited people; the telegraph offices were overwhelmed with messages

JAY GOULD, Esq.

ordering sales, or purchases of gold or stocks; and the whole nation was watching eagerly to see what the result of this convulsion was to be. All trade was stopped, and even the president felt that it was time to raise his hands. No one who has not seen the New York Gold Room can understand the spectacle it presented; now a perfect pandemonium, now silent as the grave. Fisk, in his dark back office across the street, with his coat off, swaggered up and down, a "big cane in his hand," and called himself the Napoleon of Wall street. He really believed that he directed the movement, and while the street outside imagined that he and Gould were one family, and that his purchases were made for the clique, Gould was silently flinging away his gold at any price he could get for it.

Whether Fisk really expected to carry out his contract, and force the bears to settle, or not, is doubtful, but the evidence seems to show that he was in earnest, and felt sure of success. His orders were unlimited. "Put it up to 150," was one which he sent to the Gold Room. Gold rose to 150. At length the bid was made—"160 for any part of five millions," and no one any longer dared take it. "161 for five millions,"—"182 for five millions." No answer was made, and the offer was repeated,—"162 for any part of five millions." A voice replied, "Sold one million at 62." The bubble suddenly burst, and within fifteen minutes, amid an excitement without parallel even in the wildest excitements of the war, the clique brokers were literally swept away, and left struggling by themselves, bidding still 160 for gold in millions which no one would any longer take their word for; while the premium sank rapidly to 135. A moment later the telegraph brought from Washington the government order to sell, and the result was no longer possible to dispute. Mr. Fisk had gone too far, while Mr. Gould had secretly weakened the ground under his feet.

Gould, however, was saved. His fifty millions were sold, and although no one yet knows what his gains or losses may have been, his firm was now able to meet its contracts and protect its brokers. Fisk was in a very different situation. So soon as it became evident that his brokers would be unable to carry out their contracts, everyone who had sold gold to them turned in wrath to Fisk's office. Fortunately for him it was protected by armed men whom he had brought with him from his castle of Erie; but, nevertheless, the excitement was so great that both Mr. Fisk and Mr. Gould thought it best to retire as rapidly as possible, by a back entrance leading into another street, and to seek the protection of the Opera House. There was nothing but an army could disturb them; no civil mandate was likely to be served without their permission within these walls, and few men would care to face Fisk's ruffians in order to force an entrance.

CHAPTER V.

CONCLUSION OF THE GOLD CONSPIRACY—FISK'S ACCOUNT OF HIS INTERVIEW WITH CORBIN—THE WHOLE STATEMENT PRONOUNCED A HUMOROUS FICTION—HIS OWN ACCOUNT OF HIS INRERVIEW WITH GOULD—FICTION NO. 2—ROBBING OF BONNER BY GOULD—TAKING POSSESSION OF THE SUSQUEHANNA RAILWAY—REPLACING SUSQUEHANNA MEN WITH ERIE MEN BY THE SHERIFF—NEW CHARACTER OF ADMIRAL OF THE FALL RIVER STEAMERS—INTRIGUES WITH MISS MANSFIELD AND OTHERS—LEGAL PROCEEDINGS, ETC.

The subsequent winding-up of this famous conspiracy may be stated in a few words. But no account could possibly be complete which failed to reproduce in full the story of Mr. Fisk's last interview with Mr. Corbin, as told by Fisk himself:

I went down to the neighborhood of Wall street, Friday morning, and the history of that morning you know. When I got back to our office, you can imagine I was in no enviable state of mind, and the moment I got up street that afternoon I started right round to old Corbin's to rake him out. I went into the room and sent word that Mr. Fisk wanted to see him in the dining-room. I was too mad to say anything civil, and when he came into the room, said I, "You damned old scoundrel, do you know what you have done here, you and your people." He began to wring his hands, and, "O !" he says, "this is a horrible position. Are you ruined?" I said I didn't know whether I was or not; and I asked him again if he knew what had happened? He had been crying, and said he had just heard; that he had been sure everything was all right; but that something had occurred entirely different from what he had anticipated. Said I, "That don't amount to anything; we know that gold ought not to be at 31, and that it would not be but for such performance as you have had this last week; you know damned well it would not if you had not failed." I knew that somebody had run a saw right into us, and said I, "This whole damned thing has turned out just as I told you it would." I considered the whole party a pack of cowards, and I expected that when we came to clear our hands they would sock it right into us. I said to him, "I don't know whether you have lied or not, and I don't know what ought to be done with you." He was on the other side of the table, weeping and waiilng, and I was gnashing my teeth. "Now," he says, "you must quiet yourself." I told him I did not want to be quiet. I had no desire to ever be quiet again, and probably never should be quiet again. He says, "But, my dear sir, you will lose your reason." Says I, "Speyers (a broker employed by him that day) has already lost his reason; reason has gone out of everybody but me." I continued. "Now what are you going to do? You have got us into this thing, and what are you going to do to get out of it?" He says, "I don't know. I will go and get my wife." I said, "Get her down here." The soft talk was all over. He went up stairs and they returned, tottling into the room, looking older than Stephen Hopkins. His wife and he both looked like death. He was tottling just like that. (Illustrating by a trembling movement of his body.) I have never seen him from that day to this.

This is sworn evidence, before a committee of congress; and its humor is perhaps the more conspicuous because there is every reason to believe that there is not a word of truth in the story from beginning to end. No such interview ever occurred, except in the unconfined apartments of Mr. Fisk's imagination. His own previous statements make it certain that he was not at Corbin's house at all that day, and that Corbin did not come to the Erie offices that evening, and again the next morning. Corbin himself denies the truth of the account without limitation; and adds that when he entered the next morning Fisk was there. "I asked him how Gould felt after the great calamity of the day before." He remarked, "O, he has no courage at all. He has sunk right down. There is nothing left of him but a heap of clothes and a pair of eyes." The internal evidence of truth in this anecdote would support Mr. Corbin against the world.

In regard to Mr. Gould, Fisk's graphic description was probably again inaccurate. Undoubtedly the noise and scandal of the moment were extremely unpleasant to this silent and impenetrable intriguer. The city was in a ferment, and the whole country pointing at him with wrath. The machinery of the Gold Exchange had broken down, and he alone could extricate the business community from the pressing danger of a general panic. He had saved himself, it is true; but in a manner which could not have been to his taste. Yet his course from this point must have been self-evident to his mind, and there is no reason to suppose that he hesitated.

His own contracts were all fulfilled. Fisk's contracts, all except one, in respect to which the broker was able to compel a settlement, were repudiated. Gould probably suggested to Fisk that it was better to let Belden fail, and to settle a handsome fortune upon him, than to sacrifice something more than $1,000,000 in sustaining him. Fisk, therefore, threw Belden over, and swore that he had acted only under Belden's order; in support of which statement he produced a paper to the following effect:

SEPTEMBER 24.

DEAR SIR: I herely authorize you to order the purchase and sale of gold on my account during this day to the extent you may deem advisable, and to report the same to me as early as possible. It is understood that the profits of such order are to belong entirely to me, and I will, of course, bear any losses resulting. Yours,

WILLIAM BELDEN.

JAMES FISK, JR.

This document was not produced in the orignal, and certainly never existed. Belden himself could not be induced to acknowledge the order; and no one would have believed him if he had done so. Meanwhile the matter is before the national courts, and Fisk may probably be held to his contracts; but it will be far more difficult to execute judgment upon him, or to discover his assets.

One of the first acts of the Erie gentlemen after the crisis, was to summon their lawyers, and set in action their judicial powers.

The object was to prevent the panic-stricken brokers from using legal process to force settlements, and so render the entanglement inextricable. Messrs. Field and Shearman came, and instantly prepared a considerable number of injunctions, which were sent to their judges, signed at once, and immediately served. Gould then was able to dictate the terms of settlement; and after a week of complete paralysis, Broad street began, at last, to show signs of returning life. As a legal curiosity, one of these documents, issued three months after the crisis, may be reproduced, in order to show the power wielded by the Erie managers:

Supreme Court. H. N. Smith, Jay Gould, H. H. Martin, and J. B. Bach, plaintiffs, against John Bonner and Arthur L. Sewell, defendants. Injunction by order.

It appearing satisfactorily to me by the complaint duly verified by the plantiffs that sufficient grounds for an order of injunction do exist, I do hereby order and enjoin * * * That the defendants, John Bonner and Arthur L. Sewell, their agents, attorneys, and servants, refrain from pressing their pretended claims against the plaintiffs, or either of them, before the arbitration committee of the New York Stock Exchange, or from taking any proceedings thereon, or in any relation thereto, except in this action.

GEORGE G. BARNARD, J. S. C.

NEW YORK, Dec. 29, 1869.

Mr. Bonner had practically been robbed, with violence, by Mr. Gould, and instead of his being able to bring the robber into court as the criminal, the robber brought him into court as criminal, and the Judge forbade him to appear in any other character. Of all Mr. Field's distinguished legal reforms and philantropic projects, this injunction is beyond doubt the most brilliant and the most successful.

THE SUSQUEHANNA WAR.

Shortly after the explosion of Black Friday, Fisk and Gould conceived the idea of seizing, *vi et armis*, the Albany & Susquehanna railway, to make it a branch and feeder of the Erie. The account of the war of injunctions and receiverships, which culminated in Fisk s assuming command of a regiment of Erie employees, and setting forth to take armed possession of the road, is too lengthy for publication in these pages.

The Barnard receivers were thus fairly installed in possession of the Binghampton end at the road, of the point where it connected with the Erie. An Assistant Superintendent of the Erie railway was at once appointed Superintendent of the Albany & Susquehanna, and a conductor of the same road was ordered to take out the regular train to Albany, which was still standing at the platform where it was seized. Matters were evidently approaching a crisis. Different sets of receivers were operating the two ends of the road, and two sheriffs, bearing conflicting processes, were rapidly approaching each other on trains drawn by the locomotives and directed by the officers of the hostile factions. This condition of affairs was telegraphed to the Ramsey train at Harpersville, twenty-five miles from Binghampton, and, after some consideration, it was determined to proceed no further. Meanwhile the news of the Binghamton proceedings caused Superintendent Van Valkenburg to decide on vigorous measures. In the first place he proceeded to clear the offices of all hostile influences. Mr. Fisk had not that day been allowed within the premises. Repeatedly, in company with the sheriff and others, had he presented himself, and energetically demanded admission. It was of no avail. It was different with Mr. Courter, his fellow receiver; he had been treated with a degree of courtesy, and, indeed, had been permitted to sustain the character of a nominal receiver within the offices. This gentleman was, however, now notified by Mr. Van Valkenburg that the farce of a double possession was to terminate then and there. On Saturday, in the little unpleasantness with Mr. Fisk, Van Valkenburg had given some indications that he was a man of few words and decided action. The hint had not been thrown away. Mr. Courter, after a formal resistance just sufficient to establish the fact of forcible ejectment, withdrew from the premises, and the Barnard receivers abandoned every pretence of actual possession of the Albany end of the line. Van Valkenburg's next move was to telegraph an order over the road, stopping every train where it then was; all movement was thus brought to a stand. An extra train, carrying 150 men from the workshops, under command of the master mechanic, was then sent up the road to be ready for any emergency. Having thus cleared everything away for action, the next move of the other side was in order.

The representatives of this other side were meanwhile advancing from the opposite direction ; upon the train were the sheriff of Broome county, the Erie superintendent of the road, and some twenty men. As they moved along, the orders of Judge Barnard were served at each way station, the old officials of the road were displaced, and Erie men were substituted for them. So eager, indeed, was the sheriff in the discharge of his duties, under the electro-writ of assistance, that he not only served an order, the illegal character of which he must have more than suspected, throughout his own county, but he continued to do so throughout the adjacent county, and, indeed, seemed not indisposed to extend his bailiwick to Albany. At Afton, about thirty miles from Binghampton, a despatch was received from Mr. Van Valkenburg, notifying the party that any farther advance would be at its own peril. The Albany people were then lying at Bainbridge, six miles farther down the track. After some hesitation, which involved a great deal of rapid telegraphing and no inconsiderable delay, positive orders for an advance came to the Erie party, followed shortly after by reinforcements. It was now deep in the night, but the train at last was started, and moved slowly and cautiously toward Bainbridge. The Albany party was prepared to receive it. They lay on a siding, with a patent frog—a little machine made to slide trains on to the rails, but equally calculated to slide them off—attached at a convenient point to the main track. In total ignorance of this bit of strategy, the Erie people felt their way along, when, just as Bainbridge, to their very great relief, seemed safely reached, their locomotive gently and suddenly glided off the track, and their train was brought to a standstill. The instant this took place the Albany train moved up the siding, passed triumphantly by its disabled opponents and on to the main track above them, where it took its position in the rear, effectually cutting off all retreat. As the Erie party tumbled out of their train, they were met by Mr. Smith, one of the counsel of their opponents, who glanced at the process under which they were acting, and at once pronounced it worthless. There was no alternative; they had fallen into a trap, unconditional surrender was all that remained. This was accordingly submitted to, and Sheriff Browne, of Broome county, and all his *posse comitatus*, were helped off their train, and duly served with the order of Judge Peckham, restraining them from doing or attempting anything in aid of the receivers appointed by Judge Barnard.

Having disposed of this little party by capture, and it being now broad day, the Ramsey commander decided vigorously to follow up his advantage, steaming up the road toward Binghamton. On the way he displaced the recently-appointed Fisk men, and replaced the ejected Ramsey men in charge of the various stations. Everything proceeded well until the train approached the long tunnel, near Binghamton. This was the battle-ground chosen by the Erie party.

Here, close to their base of operations, and near their supplies, they had massed their reserves, after the total and ignominious capture of their advance guard.

The tunnel is some 2,200 feet in length, and is about fifteen miles from Binghamton. It marks the last summit the road crosses in going west, and, on either side, is approached by a heavy ascending grade and round a sharp curve. The Albany party arrived at this point at about 10 o'clock, and here halted. On the other side of the hill, trains were bringing up workmen from the Erie shops, under the officers of the Erie road, until Mr. Fisk's threat in regard to "any number of men" seemed tolerably certain to be verified. It was a motley collection, the control of which must have considerably puzzled the General Superintendent of the Erie railway, who found himself in command. A more unwieldy body could not well have been got together. The men were wholly unarmed, except, perhaps, with sticks, which one party was detailed to cut in the neighboring wood; they had been hastily summoned from the shops, and were as ignorant as children of the errand they were about, nor had they the slightest enmity toward those opposite to whom they stood in ludicrous array. This, however, was not the case with the Susquehanna people. They were now thoroughly stirred up and ready for anything. Most of them had for years been in employ of the road, and many were personally attached to Mr. Ramsey; they regarded the effort to dispossess him as aimed also at themselves. They were, too, flushed with the success at Bainbridge, and possessed with a strong *esprit de corps*. Such being the opposing elements, they lay waiting for peremptory orders, which, in any case, had to come from Albany, for there both Fisk and Van Valkenburg kept their headquarters. From time to time reinforcements came up, until by 7 o'clock the Erie party was raised to an unwieldy mob of some 800 men, while their opponents numbered hardly less than 450. The Erie people decided now to try an advance, and accordingly a train well loaded with combatants was set in motion. It moved slowly through the tunnel and emerged safely from the eastern end, merely having to replace a single rail. This done, the advance was continued. Meanwhile the Albany people were fully notified of the impending danger. Accordingly, when the Erie people had replaced the rail and started, they started too, and thus the first intimation the raiders had of danger was the discovery, on rounding the sharp curve, of an approaching locomotive, angrily puffing up the grade, and apparently bent on mischief.

This was more than they were prepared for. Their whistle at once signalled danger, which the Albany locomotive replied to by signalling to them to get out of the way. In vain the Erie conductor jumped off his train and gesticulated like a madman; in vain the Erie engineer tried to back out of the way; the curve was here so sharp and the incline up which it was necessary to back in order to return into the tunnel was so great, that it was instantly evident, not only that the Albany people wanted a collision, but that their wish was to be gratified. Though the Erie engine could not reverse, it had stopped, and the heavy grade kept down the speed of the Albany train, so that the collision rather indicated an *animus* than inflicted an injury, nevertheless, in a moment the two locomotives came together with a sharp shock. The damage done was not great; guards and cow-catchers were swept away, head-lights were broken, and the attacking locomotive was roughly thrown from the track; but the collision of engines was the signal for a collision of men. Before the trains had met they were emptied of their loads. Such a system of opposition was something on which the Erie people had not counted, and when, similtaneously with the collision, the Albany men rushed upon them with loud shouts, they were at once completely demoralized, and broke into a precipitate flight. Their locomotive, with broken lights and a pistol bullet through its cab, vigorously reversed, until it had reversed itself out of the *melee* and into the tunnel, while they themselves took to their heels and scampered back toward Binghamton. A few remained on board the train, a few stumbled back through the darkness of the tunnel, but the greater part to whom their terror perhaps lent wings scaled the mountain like a sand-hill in their flight.

Since the conclusion of the Susquehanna war, in which he was signally worsted, Fisk's appearance on the stage has been alternately in the character of "Admiral" of the Fall River line of steamers, paramour of Miss Josephine Mansfield and sundry harlots of the *opera bouffe*, and buffoon of the New York press. He will offend neither the stockholders of the Erie railway, nor public decency any longer.

The initial proceedings against James Fisk, jr., which have constituted a part of the reform measures in New York, have been stayed by the sudden removal of the defendant to a higher bar. A bold, bad man has come to a stop in his carreer by the hand of an assassin, and the honest people of New York, and of the entire country, will breathe more freely now that he has gone. The manner of his death could not have been unexpected to his friends, if he had any friends. No man can lead such a life of fraud and debauchery without exposing himself, at every step, to the vengeance of some one of his victims. Such a fate is inevitable, and only points to the old truth, that crime brings at last its own punishment. There will be no sympathy felt for the deceased by right-minded persons, while there may be a regret that the law was not sufficiently powerful to protect the community and vindicate itself, by punishing him to an extent commensurate with the enormity of his career. Nothing in his public or private life will call for any regret that he has gone. There was so much of seeming success attaching to his career, so much of a certain brilliancy and joility about his intrigues, and so much of audacity in every step that he took, whether pursuing a mistress or plotting against the very life of the commercial institutions of the country, that unthinking men began to imagine that his assurance was omnipotent, and could bend everything to its own base purposes. It had already begun to debauch public sentiment. Allured by the success of Fisk, young men had come to regard him as an admirable Crichton in finance, and he had plenty of imitators. Nemesis has come none too soon to the defence of public morality, and it has come in just the manner that might have been expected. It was fitting that he should die in the same disgraceful manner as he had lived, and at the hands of the paramour of his own mistress.

While there will be little regret on the one hand at the death of Fisk, there will be no sympathy on the other expressed for the assassin Stokes. It was the act of a coward in every particular. The murderer was the counterpart of the murdered. He only lacked the opportunities and the money to be as great a scoundrel. The two men up to the time that Fisk introduced Stokes to Mansfield, had run a parallel course of vice, and shared in the common results of their operations *pro rata*. They had embarked in the amusement business simply for purposes of profligacy, and the queens of *opera bouffe* and the *danseuses* of the spectacular stage were the inmates of the disgusting harems which these men established. In an unlucky moment, Fisk introduced Stokes to his mistress, Mrs. Mansfield, and the latter supplanted him in her affections. From that moment Fisk bent all his efforts to crush his rival, and in this strife met his death. Stokes was not lacking in any of the qualities which marked his rival, but they seemed more vulgar because they had not the lustre of Fisk's gold. Stokes was the Bill Sikes of the drama. Fisk the Jew.

Both of them were gamblers, blackmailers, swindlers and debauchees. Stokes fleeced the unwary by every artifice known to the green cloth; Fisk, by every trick known to the thieves of railways. Stokes blackmailed individuals unknown to fame; Fisk blackmailed bankers, judges, and juries. Stokes swindled small men; Fisk swindled great corporations. In debauchery, Stokes proved himself the stronger of the two, for he carried off Fisk's own mistress so effectually that not even his gumshoes were allowed a place in her apartments. He proved himself a coward, as all such men do; and, sneaking up behind his victim, shot him before he could have an opportunity to defend himself. While the one deserved his death, the other deserves the halter. Justice will not be avenged of herself until the assassin follows in the steps of his victim, and the woman Mansfield is driven to her proper place by public sentiment.

The court before whom he has been called is incorruptible; the witnesses who will rise in swift array against him cannot be suborned. His life was a positive injury to the whole community, corrupting in its influences, and blighting everything of good with which it came in contact. While his murderer lives, however, the vindication of justice is not complete. They were partners in vice. United in life, they ought not to be long divided in death. When the assassin Stokes has expiated his crime a long step will have been taken in the great reform which the honest indignation of the public has demanded. The axe will have been laid at the root of the tree, and the smaller rogues of every hue, who have flourished upon the vices of those two men, will disappear with that which gave them support and encouragement. Vulgar and brutal as the instrument may have been which perpetrated this deed, and speedy as should be the punishment for it, it nevertheless teaches the salutary lesson to the young men of this country, that the way of the transgressor is hard; and that, in their efforts to get rich, virtue, honor, and manliness are not yet so old-fashioned as not to pay better than the vice, dishonesty, and lust which have marked the career of the late James Fisk, jr.

CHAPTER VI.

Col. Fisk's Death—Lying in State in the Opera House—
Crowds of Curiosity Seekers—Order of the Ceremonies
—Arrival at Brattleboro—Grief of the Mourners—An
Actress' Last Tribute—The Interment.

We have traced the career of James Fisk, jr., through his varied and eventful course, marking its imperfections without prejudice, pointing to its errors with no pharisaical self-righteousness, and only asking as our reward that this hastily prepared sketch of a life that was worse than thrown away, since all the influences which it exerted were evil and vile—all the workings of the undisciplined mind that controled it were base and sensual, and degrading, may serve as a warning to the inexperienced, and that in its terrible and sudden ending they may see how, soon or late, a retribution proportionate to his crimes will be visited upon the offender by Him who, looking through the flimsy cloak of wealth and position which screened them from all earthly tribunals, and in the grand, calm, strong majesty which maketh "a thousand years as a day," declares "vengence is mine. I will repay." Over the record of his last hours the pen moves slowly, as if the hand that guided it shrunk from its sad task—as if the brain hesitated at its work of dictating the words, " he has gone unprepared into eternity." No wonder the blood creeps slowly and chilly back to hearts that ache for him—no wonder his fair young wife plead with voice choked with her sorrow, " Oh, my Father, if it be *possible* let this cup pass from me,"—adding in her dispair, "if you *must* take him, oh, take his soul too to yourself." But never yet was the stern messengers purpose stayed, or his work left undone at the pleadings of those on whom the stroke fell more heavily than upon the victim, and in a few short hours it was said of him, " Fisk is dead," and public opinion stood hat in hand with obsequeous reverence, while the funeral procession passed by with its magnificent display, bearing its unconscious, but gorgeously arrayed burden, to its last resting place. White hands scattered flowers over the coffin, and their drooping petels and dying odors were a tribute rather to the affection of the giver, than to the worth or virtue of him over whom they faded. It is said that a popular actress of New York, laid over his pulseless heart, a wreath of *Immortelles*—and in that last act this beautiful, but unrepentant magdalene declared to the world, and to the stricken and bereaved wife and family, the relations which had existed between the dead man, lying in state before her, and herself. No more significant but humiliating commentary could have been made upon his life, than the class of people who mourned him as a friend.

An immense and boisterous crowd of excitement-seekers and unthinking admirers of James Fisk, jr., assembled on Monday, Jan. 8th, at the Grand Opera House, New York, to witness the last dazzling scenes in the erratic and brilliant career of the dead Prince of Erie. For blocks around the place was packed with a tumultuous and struggling mob, which it required the utmost exertions of the police to restrain. So questionable was the aspect of these throngs, that it was deemed unsafe to trust them within the Opera House where the dead man lay in state in his fine gorgeous Colonel's uniform. Only the privileged few were admitted, and after the reading of the Episcopal burial service, the coffin was removed to a plumed hearse, and accompanied to the New Haven depot by 200 musicians, the Ninth Regiment, the Erie employes, and a number of carriages containing relatives and friends. The crowds that watched the passing procession ceased their chatting and laughing for a moment, but turned gaily away at its close to seek the next sensation.

The vast throng of human beings which swayed and surged to and fro before the Grand Opera House and Fisk's residence, seemed impressed with the one idea, that Fisk in death was to be as amusing and ostentatious as in life, and that the promised funeral pageant was to be, as much as its solemn character would permit, in keeping with the parades, serenades and speeches with which he was wont in life to regale the multitude. The crowd before the buildings at 12 o'clock numbered 25,000 people, mostly men of that doubtful class whose delight it had been to repeat Fisk's latest witicism, to attend his regimental parades, and to gossip concerning his amours with notorious women. They never spoke of him as " Col. Fisk," to whom they had paid deference as a brave and honorable man; nor as Mr. Fisk, the financier, whose ability they had admired. It was the " Jim " Fisk of the Opera Bouffe and Mansfield fame, and litigous notoriety; the

"Jim" Fisk of the multitude, whom they knew, and the name was as familiar in the mouths of blackguards as though they spoke of an intimate associate whose life had been, like most of their own careers, a warfare against society and law.

The shouting and struggling of the crowd below could be heard plainly by the military guard and civilians grouped around the body of Fisk in the lobby of the Erie railroad offices. The showy coffin, liberally adorned with gold-plated ornaments, rested on two low stands, and in this, garbed in the gold-laced uniform of the colonel of the Ninth, lay Fisk, his moustache carefully waxed, white kid gloves on his hands, and his feet buried under white flowers, in various devices. The unnatural pallor which came immediately after death had given way to his ordinary complexion, and his features were not distorted in the slightest degree. Officers of the 9th, 8th, and other regiments of the Third brigade stood about the coffin, and in the offices opening from the lobby a number of ladies, handsomely, and in some instances magnificently attired, wept and discussed their former associate. On the corridor over-looking the lobby a number of the attaches of the Opera House, of both sex, looked down on their late patron. Some of them indulged in spasmodic fits of weeping, but chatted freely in the intervals of their lamentation.

At 1 o'clock a few of the "public" were admitted, but the rush soon became too heavy, and the door was closed against strangers. At 1 1-2, Chaplain Flagg, of the Ninth regiment, began to read the Episcopal burial service. During this, Fisk's mother, wife and sister entered, accompanied by gentlemen, and sat during the remainder of the exercises near the coffin. When the services were finished, Fisk's relatives gazed on his face, and the three ladies kissed him. The Ninth regiment, with its band, the Aschenbrodel society, and the Erie railroad and Opera house employes then filed past the coffin and looked at the corpse.

While the body of the murdered man was lying in state at the Grand Opera House, a few of the coryphees who had been the recipients of his kindness and favor, were gathered in one of the corridors, with clenched fists and streaming eyes swearing vengeance upon the assassin if he should ever be so fortunate as to escape the clutches of the law.

Just before the coffin-lid shut out forever the pale calm face of the victim of insane fury from the sight of them who had loved him, a well-known and popular actress advanced to the casket and placed a wreath of immortelles upon the lifeless remains of her frend.

THE PROCESSION TO THE DEPOT—FISK FOLLOWED BY HIS ERIE RETAINERS.

The coffin of the dead Erie magnate was closed at about two o'clock, wrapped in the United States flag, and borne to the hearse through the Twenty-third street doorway, the chaplain and many officers of the 9th Regiment walking in advance. The 9th Regiment was waiting on the south side of Twenty-third street, the right resting on Eighth avenue. The rigimental band and the Aschenbrodel Verein played an impressive dirge as the coffin was carried out. The procession then moved in the following order :

· First came about 100 police, and next the band of the Ninth, playing the "Dead March in Saul." Employes of the Erie Railroad followed, about 1 000 strong. Then came the Ninth in triple line, with arms reversed. The soldiers wore no emblem of mourning, but the civilians had crape on their left arms. The drums of the regiment were muffled, and the standards draped in black. The hearse, which came next, was decked with black and white plumes, and drawn by four black horses. The pall bearers were Col. Emmons Clark of the Seventh Regiment, Col. George D. Scott of the Eighth Regiment, Col. William B. Allen of the Fifty-fifth Regiment, Col. Frank Sterry of the Sixth Regiment, Col. Josiah Porter of the Twenty-second Regiment, and Lieut. Col. A. P. Webster of the First Regiment.

Fisk's favorite black horse, strikingly adorned, held the next position, and was led by a tall colored groom. A pair of spurred boots were fastened in the stirrups of the empty saddle, with the toes turned backward. The officers of the Third Brigade and another detachment of Erie employes followed, preceding a line of carriages containing relatives and near friends. Jay Gould, F. A. Lane and Mortimer Smith were in the leading carriage.

The procession moved through Twenty-third street to Fifth avenue, and thence through Twenty-sixth street to the New Haven depot. Three passenger cars and one baggage car, forming the regular 3 o'clock train, were in waiting. These cars were all decorated with black and white drapery, so that the ordinary passengers were involuntary mourners. The coffin was deposited in the baggage car, and a few minutes before 3 o'clock, the four cars were drawn out of the depot and up Fourth avenue on their way to Brattleboro.

Beside the relatives and nearest friends, a guard of honor from the Ninth attended the remains.

THE INTERMENT.

Upon the arrival of the funeral cortege in Brattleboro', the scene was exceedingly mournful and impressive. The sermon of Dr Flagg, which was entirely extemporaneous, was listened to with the most profound attention. The delivery was eloquent and graceful. Everybody seemed to think it went right to the point. The officers of the Ninth were in raptures over it, and Mrs. Fisk was so pleased that she called Dr Flagg to her and expressed her thanks in person. Dr. Flagg then read the solemn burial service of the Episcopal church, after which the relatives were permitted to come forward and take a last look upon the remains. It was at first intended to dispense with this painful ceremony, and Mrs. Fisk had agreed to it, but Mrs. Hooker insisted on seeing her dead brother's face once more, and the original programme was changed. The scene now was an extremely mournful one. Mrs. Hooker broke forth into loud lamentations, and her husband, unable to contain himself, followed her example. Mrs. Fisk leaned over and glued her lips to the face of the corpse for the space of several minutes. She had to be removed by gentle force, and half carried to her pew. Mr. Moore wept like a child. Mrs. Morse's grief was of the most violent character, and the two Misses Morse almost fainted from exess of feeling. The other relatives buried their faces in their handkerchiefs and sobbed audibly. Col. Fisk's colored servant rocked to and fro in his anguish. The officers of the Ninth all had their handkerchiefs to their eyes. Serg't Caspel, standing at the head of the coffin, allowed his tears to roll down unrestrained, while Adj't. Allien faced about to hide his grief. The ministers on the altar showed visible emotion, and the choir cried as though a dear relative was lost to them. This wide sorrow grew infectious and spread all over the church. People attempted to gulp down their rising tears, and then broke down into weeping and sobbing. There was not a dry eye in the building; for a second or two everybody seemed paralyzed.

Then the undertaker stepped quietly forward and let down the lid of the casket—not, however, before Adjutant Allien had secured the wreath which rested upon the colonel's body. These he stripped of their flowers, and going around among the friends and relatives presented each with a blossom as a souvenir. It was a pretty act, done on the inspiration of the moment, and one for which the adjutant received unnumbered hearty blessings. Mr. Merrit then locked the casket forever, and the battle-flag of the Ninth having been spread over its top, the following pall-bearers advanced and seized the gold-plated handles: Lieut. Col. Braine, Maj. Hitchcock, Col. W. E. Van Wyck, and Capts. Miller, Spencer and Barrows. Slowly they bore it to the street, and deposited it in the hearse-sleigh in waiting. Then forming themselves as a guard of honor around the hearse, the officers of the Ninth moved slowly down the street and took a position at the head of the procession. An immense crowd who could not obtain admission into the church, covered the postoffice steps and the sidewalk opposite. Behind the officers the steamboat men fell into line, and behind them came the civilian friends of the dead colonel. The ladies and the relatives entered ten large two-horse sleighs and followed. The first sleigh was occupied by Mrs. Fisk, Mrs. Hooker, Mr. Moore and Col. Hooker, and the second by the Misses Morse and Mrs Morse. At half-past 2 the procession started; the church bell began to toll at the same moment. A line of people half a mile long walked on either side forward. They went bearing to the right when they reached the Brattleboro' House. The windows of every residence were filled with spectators. Around the Brattleboro' House, to the left, the pageant took another turn, and began clambering up a long, steep hill. The ground was icy and covered with caked snow, which rendered locomotion difficult. The bell still tolled mournfully, and the sad procession of people followed slowly after. A number of other sleighs, owned by residents of the neighborhood, joined in behind. Up, up the winding hill-path for five minutes more and the suffering multitude were on the top.

The journey now lay along a level road, with the well-filled cemetery on the left. About the centre of the white picket fence which surrounded the resting-place of the dead, the head of the funeral turned in through an open gateway, and, by a circuitous road, arrived at a new made grave on the very edge of the burial ground. The people already surrounded the grave in large numbers when the hearse drove up. The grave is on the very edge and about the centre of the declivity of the bold bluff, on the top of which the cemetary stands. Below is a deep valley, bounded on the opposite side by the Mantasket mountain, six thousand feet high, along whose base the Connecticut winds. The scenery is romantic beyond description.

The handsome case which contained the coffin on its journey from New York was quickly brought on the ground and the casket placed inside. This case is covered with black cloth and richly silver-mounted. The officers stood in a body on the right, the relations, with Mrs. Fisk and Mrs. Hooker in front. On the left of the grave the Chaplain, the Rev. Dr. Flagg, was mounted on the newly turned up sand. The multitude gathered mournfully around, and doffed their hats. The casket having been placed upon the trestle work over the grave, Dr. Flagg invoked a solemn blessing upon the assemblage, then at a signal straps were put under the coffin, and the mortal remains of James Fisk, Jr., were lowered to the bottom of the grave. In another minute, at a quarter to 3 o'clock, New York time, six spadefuls of earth, thrown in by two small boys, and hid him from the sight of the world. Col. Fisk's wife and sister were led to their sleigh in a half fainting condition. All were sobbing as though their hearts would break. It took but ten minutes to fill up the grave. Then all the mourners took their seats in large stage sleighs which had been provided for them through the kindness of Col. Miles, and were conveyed to the depot where the train was waiting them. Col. Fisk's entire uniform, sword and all, is buried with him, excepting his splendid diamond badge, which Mrs. Fisk will keep as a menento.

CHAPTER VII.

MISCELLANEOUS COMMENTS OF THE PRESS—HOW THE PUBLIC RECEIVED IT—CONDEMNATION OF THE COWARDLY DEED—CRITICISMS UPON HIS LIFE—DISAPPROVAL OF HIS IMMORALITY AND HIS BRAZEN DISREGARD OF DECENCY, ETC., ETC.

We look at the clay that covers his last resting place, and our lips whisper: "Peace to his ashes," but with our mind's eye we look away to that land "from whence no traveler returneth," and our hearts plead with his Judge, "God have mercy on his soul." In conclusion of this brief sketch, we give a few of the many but excellent criticisms that have been passed upon his brilliant but dishonorable career.

The week-old year has had its first sensation. James Fisk, jr. is dead. In whatever guise coming, his death would have attracted universal attention; but falling the victim of a cowardly assassin, the news of his taking off fell upon the public like a clap of thunder in a clear sky. Utterly unknown a few years ago, his name and career are now as familiar as the alphabet. Like a comet, with its small head and prodigious length of tail, he challenged the gaze of all, and went as suddenly as he came. No one thought of him until every eye was riveted upon him, and without a moment's warning, he shot off into the dark.

The story of his life is familiar, and the vices of his life were only eclipsed by the infamy of his assassination. He had wronged many, in purse and morals, but his murderer was not one of the number. There was something of the Robin Hood about Fisk. He was bold, generous, and good-natured, but he was utterly unscrupulous in making money, and ostentatiously immoral in spending it. A discarded mistress and her "man" thought him a good subject for the blackmailing art. They were mistaken. After a few passes at law, the blackmailers were bluffed. No sooner did Stokes find his game blocked and himself "the bitter bit," than he resolved to end all with a bullet. Had the public and private life of Fisk been spotless, the assassin's guilt would hardly have been greater, for as between those two, justice was wholly on the victim's side.

While Stokes committed a murder for which there is no extenuation whatever, it must be admitted that the loss of such a man as Fisk is gain. His methods in business were thoroughly demoralizing. He dazzled the imagination with visions of wealth gotten dishonestly His influence was powerfull in making young men impatient of the slow and irksome toilings of legitimate business. Why drudge and economize when there is a royal road, an Aladdin's lamp?

The effect was all the worse because he flaunted his success in the public face so shamelessly, and lavished his money in the gratification of coarse appetites and tastes. One hardly knows which to reprobate most, the making or the spending of his money. Had his life run on prosperously to a green old age, his career would have been a standing menace to honesty and virtue; but the dullest must now see that, without taking into account the world beyond, his life was a pitiful failure; and this is a matter of rejoicing, even in the immediate presence of death.

PISK AND THE ERIE RAILWAY.

The moralists and the biographers have had their say about the late Colonel Fisk, and now I propose, without trespassing upon their preserves, to record a few things more or less connected with him. In the first place, I must record the fact that speculation is rife as to what is to become of the Erie railroad, now that the man is gone whose reckless audacity enabled him to control it for the past few years. While Jay Gould, its president, was the subtle suggester of swindles, he had not the recklessness or the nerve—to say nothing of the total disregard of public opinion—to enable him to carry them out successfully. Jim Fisk had all these requisites, but lacked the brain to invent, and plot, and scheme. The two came together, and the thing was done. Now, the question is, What will Gould do without his right bower? It is impossible for him to find another Jim Fisk, and even if found, it would be impossible for Gould to confer upon him the authority which Fisk held by virtue of his office as treasurer, or to give him a knowledge of all the develish arts used by them to get the control of the road. Already other railroad magnates are in the field, scheming for a hold upon the throat of Erie; while the English stockholders are preparing for a still more vigorous struggle to secure their rights.

Already, and before the death of Fisk, their power was beginning to be felt, to break down the corrupt barriers which purchased Judges had thrown in their way, and Gould was beginning to weary of the fight. These stockholders have secured General Sickles as their counsel, and he has already had several interviews with the new Attorney General, General Barlow, relative to the best means of destroying the present management of Erie, and punishing the conspirators who stole it from the stockholders. He has been quietly pushing his investigations to this end since he first came ashore, and he is one of those persistent men who never give up. He has been assured of all the money necessary to carry on the struggle; and, if it is necessary, to buy up all the shares that have been issued—watered stock and all,—to secure these Englishmen their rights, the money necessary will be forthcoming.

Fisk and Gould, in order to obtain and retain control, have had to buy "proxies" on which they could vote at the elections. Indeed, they first got control of the road by giving old Daniel Drew a million of dollars for the privilege of using his ten million shares for a few months for election purposes. Since then, they have bought the "proxy" of every little shareholder they could find, and Fisk has held them tightly under his tumb. But Fisk is dead, and now other great Railway kings contest for these same "proxies" to use against Gould. The bidding is spirited, for the stake is a large one,—no less than one of the greatest arteries through which rushes the commerce of the country. Every other great artery is more or less dependent upon it, and any one of the others would like to control it. If a few of these "proxies" fall into the hands of the Englishmen, their triumph will be complete. But the Grand Trunk, the New York Central, the Pennsylvania Central, and other great lines want the control of the Erie vested in this country so, while the fight goes on to despoil Gould, an eye must be kept to windward to see that the plum does not fall into the open mouths of the Englishmen.

I have it on good authority that the owners of the shares upon which Fisk and Gould have been allowed to vote, have been dissatisfied with Fisk for some time. He was too extravagant in his expenditures, and too notorious in his private life. The loves and amours of the "Prince of Erie" were public property, and much of the discredit of them attached to Erie. These pious people were being daily scandalized; and, now that the road was virtually stolen, and they were receiving their share of the plunder, they desired to " respectableize " its future transactions. For this purpose, Fisk was not their man. So there have been wheels within wheels, and the workings of the minor ones boded no good to Fisk.

So taking all these things into consideration there is much speculation as to the future of Erie. It is safe to predict that its management will soon be changed; and the probability is, that it will be so merged into other corporations as to form a grand monopoly, and, at the same time, to greatly increase the railroad facilities of the country. Little of this struggle for supremacy will be made public, but it will go steadily on, and will have a great effect upon business transactions.

CHAPTER VIII.

ATTEMPTS OF THE PRESS TO GLOSS OVER HIS SENSUAL VILLANIES—HIS LACK OF FAITH IN WOMAN—HIS OPERA—HAREM—COMPLIANT HUSBANDS—MONEY COVERS A MULTITUDE OF SINS—HIS OWN HAND WROUGHT THE RUIN—JENKINS AND FUNERAL FLOWERS, ETC., ETC.

The assassination of James Fisk, Jr., was one of the most dastardly acts it has ever been our lot to record. Assassinations in every form are cowardly, and deserve all the reprehension and execration of which our language and our indignation are capable; but it is seldom that a premeditated murder is executed in so cowardly and contemptible a manner as was that committed by the wretched Stokes upon James Fisk, and it is impossible to characterize it as it deserves. Whatever the provocation, it could not have been sufficient to warrant an act so thoroughly imbued with sneaking, pitiless, mean and contemptible surroundings. In the events and conditions which had brought Fisk and Stokes in contact, first in friendship, and finally in the bitterest and most uncompromising opposition, there may have been much that will convince the world that Fisk was a bad man, but we must not slay bad men as we would slay mad dogs. There is no colorable justification for avenging by the steel or bullet of the assassin, real or supposed wrongs inflicted by bad or good men, and however open Mr. Fisk's conduct and habits may have been to censure, and whatever he may have done in the shape of gigantic wickedness, the " deep damnation of his taking off " cannot be abated one iota. His murder offers nothing in palliation, and those who seek to excuse it upon any grounds whatsoever are enemies of themselves and of society, and " know not what they do." That the terrible event, and the circumstances leading to it, should be possible in a christian community, such as this professes to be, should be the cause of profound alarm, and compel reflection as to the best means of averting future results from similar causes. Both Fisk and Stokes belonged to a class which has sprung up among us since the war; reckless, adventurous, unscrupulous, conscienceless men, furnished with brilliant audacity, and regardless of every barrier interposed by morality between them and their lusts, their greed of gain, and the ostentatious display of their persons, equipages, mistresses and estates, but given a certain superficial geniality and generosity of disposition, calculated to make friends.

Money, no matter how obtained, is their first object, and with money they procure all else that they may want, including the toleration, if not the respect, of the most worthy citizens. Men of this class have for ten years monopolized hereabouts offices of trust and honor, positions of dignity and importance, and filled the public eye almost to the exclusion of every contemporary in trade, politics, finance, commerce, leading social occurrences, and even in art. Handsome, heartless, vain, avaricious, and frail women have been at the bottom of their impulses, and instigated their transactions and triumphs, and they have also been the chief cause of their misfortunes—as in the case of James Fisk, jr. Providence seems to have determined that valuable lessons shall be taught this class, and the world outside, by means of terrible calamities. Of these all-powerful, wealthy, public-opinion-defying, and envied leaders in this city, nearly all have been suddenly prostrated and placed under foot within a few months, Mr. Fisk being the only one, excepting Watson, the city auditor, who has suffered death. And such a death! It has excited universal sympathy for the victim, and general hatred and contempt for him who inflicted it. It is said that the very few friends of Stokes hope that after the unparalleled excitement which has been caused by the assassination shall have measurably subsided, public opinion will react in his favor. Let them not cling to this hope. It will not be realized. The public will wish him to be hanged, and if he does not commit suicide, hanged he will be.

The papers have made some attempt to gloss over the vileness of Jim Fisk's character, by citing his generous impulses. It is right that these latter should not be forgotten. We meet so few in this life that all should be recorded, regardless of the source whence they spring. But, in justice to the living, to the rising generation, the evil that was in him, and did so much to corrupt others, should be laid bare. Fisk was a mocker at female virtue. He had no belief in its existence, but, on the contrary, boasted that woman had no jewel money could not buy. Alas! his success as a libertine gave him only too much reason to believe his own statements. Notorious himself, he sought notorious women, and, in the halo of their popularity, paraded himself. His intrigues with actresses, and with some of the *opera bouffe* singers, were things thrust into the faces of the people. He drove John Brougham from the present Fifth Avenue theatre for the sole purpose of establishing an *opera bouffe* harem, over which presided as queen his professed mistress. The sanctity of married life was invaded by him more than once, and, to their inextinguishable disgrace be it said, he found more than one complaisant husband, who was ready to accept a lucrative position on the Erie road in consideration of his wife's infidelity.

A notable instance of this kind was in the case of a beautiful Philadelphia lady whom he met at Long Branch. The lady had a good-natured husband, who permitted her to mingle freely in frivolous society. Fisk sought her, and she fell. He brought her to New York, where she now lives, and provided her husband with a nice, easy, and profitable situation on the Erie road, where he is still employed. The parents of the lady were most estimable people, who mourned the fall of their daughter as worse than her death, till finally the father died of a broken heart. His intimacy with Mrs. Mansfield would not be worth alluding to, for her character was as bad as his, were it not for the intensity of his infatuation. He not only made her rich, and gave her all she had the assurance to ask for, but even entrusted her with the dangerous secrets of his business, which she lately used to good advantage against him,

So, I say, this total want of moral principle in Fisk, the lack of which led to his assassination, should be boldly set forth. It is well to say a good word for the dead, and to strive to bury a man's fault in the grave with him. But, when a man has deliberately and defiantly scorned all the restraints of society and the law, and, by his example and his teachings done all in his power to corrupt the morals of his associates; has scoffed at virtue and courted vice, I say those acts should be recorded for the good of mankind, as one would mark the word, " Dangerous " where rotten ice was found. The same lack of principle displayed in private life characterized his business transactions, as all the world knows. He might well be generous with his ill-gotten gains, and, by his liberality, strive to atone for his misdeeds.

Fisk's career had, at any rate, nearly terminated. The new legislature of the state of New York would have removed him from the

Erie railway within two months, at most, and the divers sumptuous establishments he supported must have fallen to the ground when the vast revenues of Erie were withdrawn. Tammany was already prostrate; Erie was the next point of attack, and Erie was Fisk. Before the evil days had entirely come, Nemesis stepped in with Stokes, and the Prince of Erie departed, not without some dignity in his closing hours, and surrounded with very considerable human sympathy. On the whole, there probably never was such a career; it was to the last successful; he died rich, and with some touching circumstances of association, which show that there was something genuine about him. His wife, deeply wronged, came to his side when recognition was beyond possibility; but he had done her justice with his last testament, and coupled her name with that of his parents, to show that, after all, this prodigal son could purchase nothing more valuable with his princely means than that which the poorest of us may have,—to return to our father's house and receive the forgiveness of those we have wronged there.

When funeral flowers have been exhausted upon the dead libertine's grave the weeping Jenkins gives his tear-glands an enterprising set back, and starts for the dungeons of the Tombs, wherin, surrounded by every evidence of æsthetic cultivation, breathing costly-perfumes, raidiant in tropical gems, enshrined amid exotics, and lounging calm and impudent on the velvet of first-class rented upholstery, lies as villainous a murderer as ever waited for the hangman's hemp. Jenkins makes to this shedder of blood as profound a salaam as if he were the living Fisk; Jenkins begs the privilege of sharing his captivity; and of seeing him eat. Stokes, the gory, becomes at once Stokes the Great; and journals are there in the metropolis of this hard-headed, plain republic, that spread out, day after day, in minute detail of disgust, every word this villain utters; each separate dish furnished to his table by the nearest French cook; the cut and the color and cost of every garment placed upon his back; the form of chair on which he sits three times a day to gratify his epicurean palate; the soup, the fish, the roast, the brand of wine and favorite fruit—the very attitude in which the murderer reclines at his table as if he were a Roman of old, victorious from the amphitheatre, and crowned with laurel dipped in the blood of his victim.

The sickening attentions showered upon this man are a disgrace to private decorum and an outrage upon public decency. They are at once a commentary upon the education of one class of American journalists, and the taste, fast-growing, of one class of the American people. They foster a morbid desire to contemplate crime in its basest and vilest form; and without adding one sentiment of virtue, or honor, or uprightness to the code of popular morality, they dazzle youth with a glitter of villainy, and render crime itself attractive and glorious. Ambition is the passion of American youth; and boys who read these tributes to the present condition of a willful murderer, will impulsively applaud the criminal and ignore the crime. Fisk himself did much to render immorality popular to the young men of his time, by the brilliancy of his own success, whose every step was a newer, a bolder, and a more naive violation of accepted law, divine or human, and the pictures which the Jenkinson of the American press are now drawing of the kid-gloved, educated, and fastidious "gentleman," whose bones, of old, would have taught a moral at the cross-roads, is calculated to out-Fisk the dead in monstrousness of precept and potency of vicious example.

Fisk's career has been in all respects disastrous to the community. His enormous dishonestys have wrought mischief that cannot be calculated. The corruption of the bench by him and his associates has been perhaps the worst political evil of the time. The man was no worse personally than many others; and we doubt not that he had some good qualities. But the effect of his example has been fearful. He has been a conspicuous example of worldly success gained through dishonesty, and used for corrupt pleasure. His gorgeous displays of wealth, his open dissoluteness, the coarse fame that attached to him, have doubtless allured a host of the young into sin. His show of recklessness and joviality, and the sort of toleration which amusement at his freaks won for him, lent a gilding to his worse traits that made their influence more pernicious.

Truth requires that the facts as to the influence of such a man upon the community should be plainly spoken. But it is not necessary to dwell with bitterness on the faults of one who has gone to meet a higher judgment than man's. It is far more important to consider the faults in our society which made such a course possible to such a man, and for which the responsibility extends through the whole community. We heartily agree with this sentiment of the *Evening Mail*:

"That he should have achieved the success he did when he so constantly flaunted before the world all that other men seek to conceal; that he should have become one of the princes among our nobility of railroad barons; that he should have been permitted to ride rough-shod over law, decency, and public morals, and that his sudden fall should have sent a shock over a continent as though some great man had left a great place vacant—all this seems to us inexpressibly sad, and inclines us to forget the poor man who now is dust, and to remember the shame and the disgrace of a community in which this career was possible."

In a moral point of view James Fisk, jr., was the worst man that America ever produced. Not that he was personally a sinner above all others, but, that the influence of his public career was the worst. He set his candle upon a hill, in full view of everybody, and its deadly flame lured to destruction the moths who think the chief end of man is to make money and spend it. The snuffing out of such a candle, like the overthrow of Napoleon and Tweed, is a public blessing.

He has paid the penalty that belongs to the social crimes of which he has been guilty, while those who attacked him, are utterly ruined.

To the wife of Mr. Fisk, who is an estimable lady, and whose greatest fault seems to have been that she indulged her husband in his dashing, wild career, without exerting herself to control him as she might possibly have done,—to such a wife the telegram she received at her elegant and quiet home, on Chester square, in Boston, must have been like a blasting thunder-bolt striking on her threshold.

And as her husband has gone where the cypress casteth its shadows upon the sepulchre instead of the bower "where the woodbine twineth," her cup of sorrow will be filled with the bitterest dregs that were ever tasted by mortal lips.

CHAPTER VIII.

FISK'S HUMOR—HIS FIRST MISTAKE—MISTAKE NO. 2—LITTLE PETER—REPARTEE—GRAVE YARD FENCE—INTERVIEW WITH VANDERBILT—THE COMMODORE'S BUCKLES—SECRET HISTORY OF ERIE.

A conciousness of the power—the power which money gives one everywhere—gave him an air of easy, gracious *debonair*. A lack of self-respect led him to place himself on a level with even the lowest, vilest, and most degraded, with a jolly " hale-fellow-well-met" sort of a way which gained him the reputation of being thoroughly democratic in his views and habits, while a coarseness and dimness of perception prevented his recognizing worth or virtue superior to his own. Like many men of strong constitution and unimpaired vigor, whose physical development is far superior to their mental development, he was an incessant jester, and if his jokes sometimes lacked something of the delicacy which would have made them more presentable, they are at least far spread, and we give a few of the most popular.

FISK'S FIRST MISTAKE.

Fisk used to often tell about his first mistake in life.

Said the colonel, " When I was a little boy on the Vermont farm, my father took me up to the stable one day, where a row of cows stood in the stable."

Said he, '' James, the stable window is pretty high for a boy, but do you think you could take this shovel and clean out the stable? "

" I don't know, ' Pop,' " said James, " I never *have* done it."

" Well, my boy, if you will do it this morning, I'll give you this bright silver dollar," said his father, patting him on his head, while he held the silver dollar before his eyes.

"Good," said James, "I'll try"—and away he went to work. He tugged and pulled and lifted and puffed, and finally it was done, and his father gave him the bright silver dollar, saying:

"That's right, James, you did it splendidly, and now I find you can do it so nicely, I shall have you do it *every morning all winter !* "

MISTAKE NUMBER 2.

Fisk said his second mistake occurred in maturer years—when he first became associated with Gould in the Erie office.

" How was it? " asked Col. Rucker.

"Well," said Fisk, "Gould had some woman litigation on hand, and he came to me and said he wanted to use my name."

" What for? " said I.

"Well, Fisk," said Gould, "you know my wife is very sensitive, and you know this woman business is full of scandal. Now, you know you don't care, so just let me use your name for a week in this case."

" What was the result, Colonel? " asked Rucker.

"Result? why, by thunder, Gould used my name one week and there wasn't anything left of it. It was used up. He got it so mixed up and scandalized that I never could retain it, and I felt as if I didn't care a damn about it afterwards !"

LITTLE PETER.

Fisk's little Peter was about ten years old, and small at that. Frequently large men would come into the Erie office and " bore " the Colonel. Then he would say:

"Here, Peter; take this man in custody, and hold him under arrest until we send for him !"

CHARITY.

One day a poor, plain, blunt man stumbled into Fisk's room. Said he:

" Colonel, I've heard you are a generous man, and I've come to ask a great favor."

"Well, what is it, my good man ?" asked Fisk.

" I want to go to Lowell, sir, to my wife, and I hav'nt a cent of money in the world," said the man in a firm, manly voice.

" Where have you been?" asked the Colonel, dropping his pen.

"I don't want to tell you," replied the man, dropping his head.

" Out with it, my man, where have you been ?" said Fisk.

"Well, sir, I've been to Sing Sing State prison."

"What for?"

"Grand larceny, sir. I was put in for five years, but was pardoned out yesterday, after staying four years and one-half. I am here, hungry and without money."

"All right, my man," said Fisk kindly, "you shall have a pass, and here—here is $5. Go and get a meal of victuals, and then ride down to the boat in an Erie coach, like a gentleman. Commence life again, and if you are honest and want a lift, come to me."

Perfectly bewildered, the poor convict took the money, and six months afterward Fisk got a letter from him. He was doing a thriving mercantile business, and said Fisk's kindness and cheering words gave him the first hope—his first strong resolve to become a man.

REPARTEE.

One day Fisk was traveling to Niagara with his brother-in-law Hooker. The directors' car passed a car full of calves.

"There, colonel—there are some of your relations," said Hooker, laughing.

"Yes—relations *by marriage*, said Fisk.

CHARITY AND FUN.

One day the colonel was walking up Twenty-third street to dine with one of the Erie directors, when a poor beggar came along. The beggar followed after them, saying, in a plaintive tone, "Please give me a dime, gentlemen."

The gentleman, accompanying Fisk, took out a roll of bills and commenced to unroll them, thinking to find a half or a quarter.

"Here, man!" said Fisk, seizing the whole roll and throwing it on the sidewalk, "take the pile."

Then, looking into the blank face of his friend, he said, "Thunderation, Sam, you never count charity, do you?"

"But, great guns, colonel, there was $20 in that roll."

"Never mind," said Fisk, "I'll stand the supper to-night."

GRAVEYARD FENCE.

Somebody in Brattleboro' came down to New York to ask Fisk for a donation to help them build a new fence around the graveyard where he is now buried.

"What in thunder do you want a new fence for?" exclaimed the colonel. "Why, that old fence will keep the *dead* people in, and *live* people will keep out as long as they can, anyway!"

FISK'S LAST JOKE.

The day before Fisk was shot he came into the office, and after looking over some interest account, he shouted, "Gould! Gould!"

"Well, what?" says Gould, stroking his jetty whiskers.

"I want to know how you go to work to figure this interest so that it *amounts to more than the principal?*" said the Colonel.

FISK'S HUMOR

There was a vein of humor in Fisk which enabled him to bear up under all reverses. After he had been ruined in his first Wall street speculations, instead of setting down in despondence and gloom, as most people would have done under similar circumstances, he started off to Boston, and in the cars mingled freely in conversation, and with funny stories and puns beguiled the tedium of the journey. This trait in his character appears very prominently in the report of Fisk's evidence in a suit commenced against Vanderbilt by Fisk and Gould on behalf of the Erie railway, to recover money from Vanderbilt, and make him take back 50,000 shares of Erie stock, on the ground that the transaction was illegal. Fisk testified as follows:

AN INTERVIEW WITH VANDERBILT.

I remember an interview with Commodore Vanderbilt in the summer of 1868; I don't remember just when the first interview was; it was after I returned from Jersey; I was absent in Jersey for a lapse of time—(laughter), and on my return I made the Commodore a call —(laughter); he said several of the directors were trying to make a trade with him, and he would like to know who was the best man to trade with; I told him if the trade was a good one he had better trade with me—(laughter); he said old man Drew was no better than a batter pudding—(great laughter); Eldridge was completely demoralized, and there was no head or tail to our concern—(laughter); I said I thought so too—(great laughter); he said he had got his bloodhounds on us, and would pursue us till we took the stock off his hands—he'd be d–d if he'd keep it. I said I'd be d–d if we'd take it back; that we would sell him stock as long as he'd stand up and take it. (Great laughter.) Upon this he mellowed down—laughter—and said we must get together and arrange this matter. He said when we were in Jersey, Drew used to slip over and see him whenever he could get out from under our eyes; that he had had a good deal of talk with him, and wanted to know if a trade made with Drew and Eldridge could be slipped through our board, saying if it could, we should all be landed in the haven of peace and harmony; I told him that I should not submit to a robbery of the road under any circumstances, and that I was dumbfounded that our directors, whom I had supposed respectable men—(great laughter)—would have nothing to do with such proceedings.

Q. Is that all that was said? A. I presume not; we had half an hour's conversation, and I think I could say more than that in half an hour. (Laughter.)

THE COMMODORE'S BUCKLES.

Q. Can you give me anything more that was said? A. I don't remember what more was said; I remember the commodore put on his other shoe—(laughter); I remember that shoe on account of the buckle—(laughter); you see there were four buckles on that shoe; I hadn't ever seen any of that kind before, and I remember it passed through my mind that if such men wore that kind of shoe I must get me a pair—(great laughter); this passed through my mind, but I didn't speak of it to the commodore; I was very civil to him. (Laughter.)

Counsel—Where was Gould all this time?

Mr. Fisk—He was in the front room, I suppose; I left him there, and found him there; but I don't know where he may have been in the meantime—(laughter); the next interview was at the house of Mr. Pierrepont; Gould and I had an appointment with Eldridge, at the Fifth Avenue hotel, and as we did not find him there, we went out to see if we could find him.

Counsel—Can you give the date of that meeting? A. No, sir

Q. Can you give the week? A. No, sir.

Q. Can you give the month? A. No, sir.

Q. Can you give the year? A. No, sir; not without reference.

SECRET HISTORY OF ERIE.

Q. What reference do you want? A. Well, I shall have to refer back to the various events of my life to see just where that day comes in, and the almighty robbery committed by this man Vanderbilt against the Erie railway was the most impressive event in my life—(laughter); the meeting at Pierrepont's was a week or ten days after the first interview with Vanderbilt; Gould and I went there about nine o'clock; we stepped into the hall together; we asked if Mr. Pierrepont was in; the servant said he would see; when the servant went into the drawing-room I was very careful to keep on a line with the door so I could see in—(laughter); presently Mr. Pierrepont stepped into the hall resembling a man who wasn't in much—(laughter); I asked him if our president was there; after some thoughtfulness on his part he said he thought he was—(laughter); during this time I had moved along towards the drawing-room door, Mr. Pierrepont having neglected to invite us in. (Laughter.)

Q. Where was Gould? A. O, he was just behind me; he's always right behind at such times—(laughter)—and while he entertained Pierrepont I opened the door and stepped in—(laughter)—and found most of our directors there; I stepped up to Mr. Eldridge and told him we had been to the Fifth Avenue Hotel and did not find him; he said he knew he was not there—(laughter); I asked what was going on, and everybody seemed to wait for some one else to answer—(laughter); being better acquainted with Drew than any of the rest of them, though perhaps having less confidence in him—(laughter)—I asked him what under heaven was up; he said they were arranging the suits; I told him they ought to adopt a very different manner of doing it than being there in the night—that no settlement could be made without requiring the money of the corporation.

CHAPTER IX.

Drew's Misery—Erie Deviltries—Black Friday—The Gum Shoes—Gone Where the Woodbine Twineth—Bringing Down Railroad Fare.

DREW'S MISERIES.

He began to picture his miseries to me; told me how he had suffered during his pilgrimage, saying he was worn out and torn away from his family, and wanted to settle matters up; that he had done everything he could, and saw no other way out for himself or the company. I told him I guessed he was more particular about himself than the company, and he said well, he was—(laughter); that he was an old man, and wanted to get out of the fight and his troubles; that they were much older in such affairs than we were; I was very glad to hear him say that—(laughter),—and that it was no uncommon thing for great corporations to make arrangements of this sort; I told him if that was the case I thought our state prison ought to be enlarged—(laughter); then Eldridge, he took hold of me; he talked about his great exertions, what he had done and consummated, that there were only two dissenting voices in the board—Gould and myself —and that if we came into the matter to-morrow the company would be free and clear of litigation, and everything would be all right, as he had got the Commodore, and Work, and Schell, to settle on a price; I told him I couldn't see it I had fought that position for seven months night and day, and for seven weeks in Jersey I had hardly taken off my clothes, fighting to keep the money of the company from being robbed; and I could see no reason why we should not fight it on still. He said he didn't want to go into it, but had tried to do the best he could with Gould and myself and could do nothing, and now an arrangement had been made with Vanderbilt and it was all right and must go through that night. I said I did not believe it was legal; these lawyers were all on our side, and I wanted to see my lawyer; he said that was no good—(laughter); then Mr.

Pierrepont argued with me; he said he did not think there was any one present who was not going to derive some benefit from it; Rapallo was writing at a table; Schell was buzzing round—(laughter) —interested in getting his share of the plunder; Work was sitting on a sofa; I had nothing to say to him—(laughter)—as we were not on very good terms; Gould and I had a conversation together, and not till 12 o'clock at night, did we give our consent; I told him I did not believe the proceedings were legal; that we had no lawyers; that the lawyers there were sold to Eldridge—hook, line, and sinker—(laughter); Gould said Eldridge had paid Evarts $10,000 for an opinion, that it is was all right, and Eaton had been paid $15,000 for an opinion, and said it was legal; I told him I thought it was a queer way of classifying opinions—(laughter); Gould consented first; he said he had made up his mind to do so as the best way to get out of the matter; I told him I would consent if he did; Drew came to me with tears in his eyes and asked me to consent, and I consented.

ERIE DEVILTRIES.

Then there was some paper drawn up and passed around for us to sign; I don't know what it contained; I didn't read it; I don't think I noticed a word of it; I didn't know the contents, and I have always been glad I didn't (laughter); I have thought of it a thousand times; I don't know what other documents I signed, signed everything that was put before me (laughter); after the devil once got hold of me I kept on signing (laughter); didn't read any of them and have no idea what they were; don't know how many I signed—kept no account after the first; I went with the robbers then and have been with them ever since (laughter); after signing all the papers, I took my hat and left at once in disgust (laughter); I don't know whether we sat down or not; I know we didn't have anything to eat. (Laughter.)

Counsel—Didn't you have a glass of wine or something of that sort?

Mr. Fisk—I don't remember.

Counsel—Wouldn't that have made an impression upon you? (Laughter.)

Mr. Fisk—No, sir! I never drink (laughter). I think I left at once, as soon as I had done signing. As we went out, I said to Gould we had sold our souls to the devil. (Laughter.) He agreed to that and said he thought so too. (Laughter.) I remember Mr. White, the cashier, coming in with the check-book under his arm, and as he came in I said to him that he was bearing in the balance of the remains of our corporation to put into Vanderbilt's tomb. (Laughter.) The next interview with Vanderbilt was several days after.

Counsel—Was Gould with you?

Mr. Fisk—Yes, sir; we never parted during that war (laughter); we went to his office one morning and found his man Friday in the front room (laughter); don't know his name; it was the same man I had seen a hundred times before when I had been there with Drew; we found the Commodore in the back room; I asked him how he was getting on; he said "first-rate"—(laughter); that he had got the thing all arranged, and the only question now was whether it could be slipped through in advance; I told him that after what I had seen the other night I thought anything could be slipped through. (Laughter.) He said we would have to manage it carefully. I told him I didn't think so; that they would be careful to go it blind. (Laughter.) He said the trade had been consummated at Pierrepont's house. I said I had no doubt of it. He said it ought not to have been carried out; that Schell had got the lion's share, and some of the lawyers on the other side might have to go hungry. (Laughter.) He asked if we were conversant with the rest of the trade. I said I had no doubt the thing had been cooked up in such a manner that it could be put through. He spoke about putting Bunker and Stewart into our board, and said it would help both him and us to carry our stock, as people would say we had amalgamated, and Vanderbilt's men coming into the Erie board would strengthen the market. That was admitted, but it worked rather different from what we expected. (Laughter.) I next saw him a day or two before the prosecution was closed up. Gould thought the Commodore's losses had not been so large as represented, and asked to see his broker's account. The Commodore said he never showed anything and we must take his word. He reiterated his losses and said they were so large, because when they had got him to give his order to sustain the market the skunks had run and sold out on him. (Laughter.) As we were coming away he said, "Boys, you are young, and if you carry out this settlement there will be peace and harmony between the roads."

Previous to commencing this suit I made a tender of 50,000 shares of Erie stock to Vanderbilt. I went up to his house in company with T. G. Shearman. I received the certificates of shares from Gould and put them in a black satchel. (Laughter.) It was a bad, stormy day, so we got into a carriage and I held the satchel tight between my legs—(laughter)—knowing that they were valuable. (Laughter.) I told Shearman not much reliance could be placed on him if we were attacked, he was such a little fellow. (Laughter, in which Mr. Shearman joined.) We concurred in the opinion that it was dangerous property to travel with. (Laughter.) Might blow up. (Laughter.) We rang the bell and went in; the gentleman came down and I said: "Good morning, Commodore; I have come to tender you 50,000 shares of Erie stock, and demand back the securities and money;" he said he had had no transactions with the Erie railway company—(laughter)—and would have to consult his counsel, I told him I also demanded $1,000,000 paid him for losses he purported to have sustained; he said he had nothing to do with it—(laughter)—and I bade him good morning. (Laughter.)

I became director in the Erie railway on the 18th of October, 1867.

Counsel—You remember that date?

Mr. Fisk—I do, well. It forms an episode in my life.

Counsel—What fixes it in your mind so well?

Mr. Fisk—I had gray hairs then.

Counsel—You have gray hairs now.

Mr. Fisk—Plenty of them. And I saw more robbery the next year than I had ever dreamed of as possible.

Counsel—You saw it, did you?

Mr. Fisk—I didn't see it, but I knew it was going on. I am now a director of the Erie railway and its controller. My duty as controller is to audit all the bills; as director to manage the affairs of the corporation honestly. (Laughter.) I would like to make an apology to the court. This is the first time I have been on the stand, and I may overstep some of the rules. (Laughter.) If I do, it is wholly in ignorance. It is new business to me, and if I don't keep within the rules I ask my counsel to guide me, for I don't know when I may be imposed on. (Laughter.)

Counsel—Your lawyer will look out for you.

Mr. Fisk—Oh, I'll look out for myself. (Laughter.) Don't give yourself any trouble about that.

Counsel—You seem to be a very frank and outspoken witness. (Laughter.) A. Well, I'm not much accustomed to you fellows (laughter); I was never on the stand but once before."

Q. When was that? A. That was when I was a boy, up in the country, in a cow case. (Great Laughter.)

BLACK FRIDAY.

Mr. Fisk's explanation of his connection with the famous Black Friday gold speculations is also characteristic of the man. He said:
"When Gould found himself loaded down to the gunwales and likely to go under, the cussed fellow never said a word. He's too proud for that. But I saw him tearing up bits of paper, and when Gould snips off corners of newspapers and tears 'em up in bits, I knew there was trouble. Then I came in to help. He knows I would go my bottom dollar on him, and I said to him; Look here, old fellow! When I was a boy on a farm in Vermont, I've seen the old man go out to yoke up Buck and Brindle; he'd lift the heavy yoke on to Brindle's neck, key the bow, and then, holding up the other end, motion to old Buck to come under, and old Buck would back off and off, and sometimes before he could persuade him under the yoke would get too heavy for dad. And Gould, old fellow, Wall street won't be persuaded and the yoke is getting heavy, and here I am to give you a lift." And again in the same connection Fisk said to Corbin: "O, Gould has sunk right down under it. You won't see anything left of him but a pair of eyes and a suit of clothes."

GONE WHERE THE WOODBINE TWINETH.

"What do you mean, Colonel," said S. S. Cox to Fisk, "by the place where the woodbine twineth?" to which interrogatory Fisk responded: "You see, I was before that learned and dignified body, the Committee on Banking and Currency, and when Garfield asked me where the money got by Corbin went to, I could not make a vulgar reply, and say up a spout, but observing, while peddling through New England, that every spout of house or cottage, had a woodbine twining about it, I said, naturally enough, where the woodbine twineth."

And in the subsequent investigation which took place, his famous reply when asked were the money had gone—"Gone where the woodbine twineth"—will be remembered as long as the memorable panic itself will.

THE GUM SHOES.

And there is a plaintive humor in the well remembered expression to Stokes, after he had been dethroned by Josie: "See here, Ned, she won't even let me leave my gum shoes in the house."

In relation to his quarrel with Mrs. Mansfield, Mr. Fisk sent a characteristic letter to the *World*, of which the following is the postscript:

"P. S..—I only wish, where your article states I burst into tears, that you gave the truth. Years ago, before the world battled me so fearfully, I have a vague recollection that emotions could be aroused which would call forth tears, but that is many years ago, far back, before energy had taken such complete hold of us all, and before ambition swayed the minds of men as it now does. But the memory of those days is lasting, and I can recall that when night came a mother's hand was laid upon my head and I was taught to repeat a simple prayer, and then I heard the words, 'My son, I must put you in your little bed.' J. F., JR."

When Fisk was about ten years of age, he kept a small market stall at Bennington, Vt. One day the eminent steamboat man, Daniel Drew, came to the market with his basket on his arm. He asked young Fisk if his eggs were fresh. "You bet," replied the ingenuous boy, "pop pulled them off the vines this morning." "Give me a dozen, sonny"' replied Mr. Drew. The next stall was kept by little Eliphalet Buckram. "Is this pumpkin good, my son?" asked the venerable stock-brooker. "It is a good enough Morgan," answered the truthful child, "but, sir, if you will examine that portion concealed from too scrutinizing view, by contact with the boards forming the counter of the stall, you will see that there is a bad spot in it." "Does not that seem unbusinesslike, my child, to cry down your own wares?" asked the kind-hearted millionaire. "My sainted mother told me I must never tell a lie with my little hatchet," responded Eliphalet Buckram. The rich man was moved to tears, he took out his purse and gave Eliphalet Buckram a pat on the head and said he was a good boy. When he had gone, Eliphalet Buckram said to little James, "O James, what made you tell such a fib? You know those eggs were laid three weeks ago. You will see that I have gained a customer, and you have lost one." Well, when Eliphalet went home, his stepmother came to the door and said: "Here you are, you lazy little sneak, and you havn't sold that pumkin yet! I'll pumkin you!" And she took him in her stepmother's arms and fanned him with an ox-goad until he said that he would prefer taking his meals off the mantelpiece for the next few consecutive days to sitting down with the rest of the family. And next day Daniel Drew came into the market ("a rearin' and a tearin'," as old inhabitants say,) and said: "Where is the boy that sold me those eggs, eh?" and Jim Fisk pointed to Eliphalet and said: "There he is, sir," and Daniel Drew reinforced that boy's stepmother's ox-goad with his cane so effectually that—but never mind. So Daniel Drew bought all his garden-sass of Jim Fisk. In after-life Eliphalet Buckram set up a grocery store, and gave trust to all the poor people, and never sanded his sugar, and wouldn't qualify his rum with water; so he burst up, and the sheriff sold him out, and he went to the poor-house. But Daniel Drew kept his eye on Jim Fisk, and bye-and-bye he gave him a partnership in the Erie firm, and Jim beat him out of $4,000,000. This is not a story for good little boys. We fear it is too near the truth.

One day a journalist sent in his card. "All right," says the colonel, "let him come in;" then turning to the gentleman of the press, and said: "Well, sir, what is the news?" "But, Mr. Fisk, I came here to get the news—" "Thunderation you did, hey! Well, I wish you would only tell as much here as you go right off and tell in the newspapers. If I thought you would, I'd say, 'Here, Peter, wind up the nickel reporter and let him talk.'" "You seem very busy to-day," remarked the reporter, resorting to the drawing-out process. "Yes," said Fisk smiling, "I'm trying to find out from all these papers where Gould gets money enough to pay his income tax. He never has any money—*fact, sir!* He even wanted to borrow of me to pay his income tax last summer, and I *lent him*, and that's gone too! This income business will be the ruination of Gould." Here the venerable Daniel Drew concealed a laugh, and Gould turned clear around, so that Fisk could only see the back of his head, while his eyes twinkled in enjoyment of the colonel's fun.

There was a good deal of fuss about that time between the Erie and Central, on the reduction of fares, so the reporter asked: "What will be the end of putting down the railroad fares, colonel?" "End? Why, we haven't begun yet. We intend to carry passengers through to Chicago, before we get through, two for a cent and feed them on the way, and when old Van does the same, the public will go on his road just to spite him!" "Of course, the Erie is the best road," continued Fisk, in his Munchausen way. "It runs faster and smoother. When Judge Porter went up with me in the directors' car, last winter, we passed 200 canal boats, about a *mile apart*, on the Delaware and Hudson canal. The train went so fast that the judge came back and reported that he saw *one* gigantic canal boat *ten miles long!* Fact, sir! We went so fast the judge couldn't see the gaps." "Are the other railroads going to help you in the fight?" asked the reporter. "Why yes—and as fast as they are convinced that we are going to make a first-class fight, they say we will help you, but they want to see Vanderbilt tied fast first." Here the Colonel threw himself into his favorite attitude—leaning forward in his chair, with his elbows on his knees. Then, said he: " Do you know what these other half-scared railroad fellows remind me of?" "No, what?" "They put me in mind of the old Texas farmer whose neighbors had caught a noted cattle thief. After catching him, they tied him to a tree, hands and feet, and each one gave him a terrible cowhiding. When tired of walloping him, they left the poor thief tied to the tree, hand and foot. He remained tied up there a good while in great agony, till by-and-by he saw with delight a strange man coming along. "Who are you?" said the kindly-looking stranger. " I'm Bill Smith, and I've been whipped almost to death," said the man in a pitiful tone. "Ah, Bill Smith! and how could they whip you?', asked the sympathizing stranger. "Why, don't you see, I'm tied?" "What, tied tight?" asked the stranger, advancing to examine the ropes. " Yes, tied tight, hands and feet, and I can't move a muscle," said the thief pitifully. "Well, William, as you are tied tight, *I don't mind if I give you a few licks myself*, for that horse you stole from me," said the stranger, cutting a tremendous whip from a bunch of thorn bushes. Then he flogged him awhile, just as all these small railroad fellows would like to flog Vanderbilt when we once get him tied."

"How about Burt, and the British stockholders?" asked some one. "Damn a Britisher," said Fisk. "There is one people in the world whom I hate more than the Jews." "Who are they?" asked a bystander. "The English only, by thunder. I think if our Savior was to be crucified again, the job could be let out cheaper in London than in Jerusalem!"

CHAPTER X.

TRAITS OF CHARACTER—COMMENTS AT THE BOARD OF TRADE ROOMS.

There was probably no man living who would go farther or spend more for revenge than Mr. Fisk if he felt himself wronged; but on the other hand, no man was more kind-hearted or ready with his means when he knew he could do good and help the deserving or a friend. He was quick to appreciate a favor, and never forgot it. Great as was his race for money, he cared as little for it as any man that may be found, knowing how little contentment money in itself can give. He had not the least grain of the miser about him. His career was much more for the fun and excitement of it than for the gain. Few men in New York to-day would care so little at becoming suddenly poor. All his immense business affairs were attended to as so much play, seeming not to weigh him down in the least. With half a dozen enterprises on hand, any one of which would be all that most men would want the care of, he seemed as free from care or anxiety as a school boy, dashed off his duties with astounding rapidity, and was facetious and full of fun all the time. His Wall street enterprises, especially, he was said to go into chiefly for the fun of the thing, regarding them as a side amusement or by-play.

No being was ever more self-sufficient or self-reliant. He satisfied himself, and acted upon his own ideas. If others liked it, it was well; if they did not like it, he didn't care. Himself was the one he intended to please—not them. The one trait in which he stood almost alone was, that he seemed to want everything and everybody in his power, and trusted nobody that he could not command absolutely. He wanted to ask nothing done as a favor, but ordered it as a right to which he was entitled. He was not harsh or offensive, but the reverse, in the exercise of his power or authority; yet all about him tacitly acknowledged it. He was so perfectly affable with every one, whether of high or low degree; his manner was so full of that hail-fellow-well-met style to every one with whom he came in contact, and he was so constantly full of fun, that he was liked not a little by the army of employes and retainers that surrounded him in his Erie offices, his theatres, his regiment, and his navy.

A reporter of the *Evening Post* happening in at the Board of Trade, found the members gathered in garrulous knots here and there, as usual, discussing the prominent questions of the day. "Fisk" was the name heard oftenest. In one bevy the fire of comment and retort waxed hot, and the members disengaged themselves, one by one, from other circles of disputation and reinforced this group, standing on tiptoe to catch a glimpse of the three or four principal parties. Our reporter mounted a table between a box of flour and a sample of wheat, and got a bird's-eye and bird's-ear command of the noisy squad.

"Say what you please about his morals," were the first words caught, "Jim Fisk was a representative American." The speaker was dressed a little flashily, with a broad hat sombrero, and he smoked a meerschaum earnestly in the intervals of talk. "The country will mourn his loss," he added. "Poor Jim! I confess I admired his career."

"Then in my opinion," said the other, "you admire the career of the vilest scoundrel in America without any exception." This was a portly, confident, self-possessed man in a silk hat and gold cane, nervous and vigorous.

At this speech there was a deprecatory "Oh! Oh!" by several, and the sombrero man took the meerschaum suddenly from his mouth and said, "It's disgraceful to talk so of a dead man. He was a bold and successful business man."

Man with gold cane; "So was Captain Kidd."

A shudder in the crowd, and a little man, in black broadcloth, touched the big man on the arm and said, "See here! Col. Fisk is dead, and his body is now on the cars, going through Connecticut. *Honi soi qui mal y pense*—speak no evil of the dead."

"That's one of the foolishest maxims that ever became current," rejoined the man with the gold cane. "Bad men, like Samson, are able to do more mischief in death than in life. Now look at"—

"Well, look at him?" interrupted the meerschaum man, "look at him!—generous"

"With other people's money," suggested the big man.

"Nobody ever lived who was more active, audacious, enterprising, untiring—"

"Except Satan," suggested the other.

"Oh! Fisk is dead—dead!" exclaimed the crowd of listeners. "Don't pitch into a corpse, Colonel!"

"Fisk isn't a corpse,' responded the gentleman addressed. "He was never so alive as he is this hour. His influence for evil is larger to-day than it ever was before. The sympathy that is begotten by his strange death at the hand of a coward, causes thousands of respectable citizens to say, "Well, he was a pretty good fellow, after all" and our young men to prepare to imitate his vices. So there never was so much need to expose him aud denounce his method as there is at this moment."

Voices: "Well, give us your opinion, Colonel.

"He was the most dangerous man that has been on this continent during this century. He never scrupled at anything to accomplish his ends, and his ends were the robbery of rich men. His boldness was not equal to a highwayman's, but his profession was just the same. He seized the money of others, without a pretense of right, and then corrupted Legislatures and bribed Judges to defend him in keeping it. His acts did more to disgrace this country abroad than anything else that has ever happened."

Man with meerschaum, "I think Fisk has been slandered a good deal."

"Every bank in New York," continued the speaker, "and every railroad that terminates there, rejoices at his death, as a public blessing."

"Ah! I see," said the meerschaum man, " you would like to have Fisk belong to your church."

"No—I belong to no church. I care nothing for his religion or irreligion. What I denounce is his immorality—his reckless, shameless profligacy. He defied civilization. He made war on society. He scouted the ways of decency."

"He was no hypocrite," suggested the little man in black.

"No; and that was another of his vices. Hypocrisy would have been a virtue in James Fisk. Hypocrisy, my friend, is the blush of vice. It is a hoisting of the colors of integrity, and a display of the consciousness of turpitude. Fisk sneered at the possibility of virtue in women, or of honesty or honor in men. He did all he could to teach that self was the only thing to live for; that the moral law was a maxim to defraud the gullible with; that only fools told the truth, and only cowards abtsained from theft."

Little man—"The telegraph says his last words were: 'Good bye; I'm going home.'"

Listener in the crowd—"No, the best account declares that just before he breathed his last he clasped his bosom and said: 'Where's my diamond breast-pin!'"

The large man continued—"Fisk was not, perhaps, largely culpable for his depraved nature. God will judge him, not we. He was what his birth, education and circumstances made him. But they made him a wholesale robber; a wrangler for the possession of a concubine; a man who, robed in yellow vest and pink cravat, whirled through Broadway in a chariot with his harem, and paid them their filthy salaries in daylight! Could anything be worse than the influence of such a profligate?"

At this point the president smote the desk with his gavel, and silence and order were observed on 'Change.

CHAPTER XI.

FAILURE ON WALL STREET—AGAIN AFLOAT—PATENT RIGHT MAN—MEETS DANIEL DREW—AT HOME ON WALL STREET— HIS PART IN THE RIOT.

In 1864, Wall street effectually "cleaned him out," his earlier speculations there have produced only disaster.

For a moment (and perhaps it is the only instance in all his life) this man of singular experiences knew the keenest pangs of dispair, became pensive and introspective, and indulged a momentary meditation upon the vanity and mutability of human affairs. But it was only for a moment. His was not a spirit to sit down and acknowledge irretrievable failure. *Nil desperandum!* "Never say die!" was his motto, and it is one to which he was eminently entitled. As he sat overlooking the street of world-wide fame and gazed down upon its hurrying throng, of which but yesterday he was one, half dreaming what to do, the pangs of failure piercing him, the spectre of want glaring at him, suddenly, as if himself unconscious of his words, he blurted out: "*Wall street has ruined me, and Wall street shall pay for it!*" At the time the words seemed the weak ravings of a mind in despair—a vain boast that might well provoke a smile. But that the threat of vengeance has been well redeemed, Wall street bitterly knows and will not soon forget. Jena was not more thoroughly avenged at Sedan; the mortification of Berlin not more thoroughly atoned by Bismarck and the troops of Fatherland marching in triumph through the gates of Paris. At the moment of uttering these words he of course had as little idea as any one *how* they were to be made good. He had not the most remote conception of any plan for recuperating his broken fortune, but genius-like, confidence of a power within him to do it, though vague, was there. The threat was hardly cold upon his lips ere he bade adieu—"for a season"—to the threatened street, packed a carpet bag, which sufficed his purpose now, and started for Boston, aimless except to get away from the scene of his disaster.

On this journey to the " Hub " the victim of Wall street did not sit in moody silence, moaning to himself over his bleeding wounds but presented an unruffled surface as though everything was all right, mingled in conversation with his usual spirits and puns, and made chance acquaintances as every one does when traveling. Among those with whom he thus got to talking was a young man who seemed sorely troubled and dejected. Perhaps it was animal magnetism that threw the two together, for however calm the surface with the late operator in stocks he was probably somewhat bilious down in the depths. The two spirits naturally waxed communicative, and soon the young stranger told his story. He proved to be one of the quite numerous class of pitiable mortals that nearly everybody has seen something of—a man laboring in distress with the elephant of a patent on his hands and brain. He had invented it, got it patented, and spent all his own means and as much more as he could borrow, endeavoring to get it before the public and reap the fortune he had dreamed would surely flow to him from it. He, too, was going back to his home dejected and crest-fallen, for his enterprise had been ill-starred, his exertions and expenditures had all been in vain, and the dreams that had sustained and lured him on so long had now all vanished, and he must carry disappointment to those who had helped him. Like all men with patents, he was ready and eager to explain its great merits and value, and talk about it and nothing else as long as any one would listen. He explained its nature and utility to his fellow miserable, who listened attentively, at first because he was quite as eager to forget his own sorrows as the young patentee was to expatiate upon his, but very soon because a sudden ray of light beamed upon his vision. Mr. Fisk saw at once that the patent was of value and that the young man's dreams of the fortune there was in it had been far from baseless; but, strange to say, he did not give his new acquaintance the consolation of suspecting this new-born conviction. However, he induced the dejecting spirit to go to Boston instead of stopping at home, philanthropically encouraging him to hope that they might possibly pick up some greenhorn there who would be wheedled into giving a little something for it, and whatever he could get now would be so much clear gain of course, as he was going home to throw it up entirely. Arrived at their journey's end, the young man gladly disposed of his patent-right for a comparative trifle and went home somewhat less heavy-hearted. The purchaser that had been wheedled into buying it was not, however, so much of a greenhorn as might be. Fisk nudged the young inventor in the ribs and chuckled with him over the sharp manner in which they had duped some unwary wight, and when he had got him to feeling nicely he left him and hurried away to reap the benefit of' the large interest which he had taken good care to secure to himself. The patent was a small improvement of great utility and extensive application in machinery used in cotton and woolen mills, proved to be of immense practical and pecuniary value, and brought the new owners a handsome income.

The downward tide in Mr. Fisk's fortune was stemmed. Confidence and courage were replenished, and with the possession once more of capital sufficient for quite extensive operations on a margin, his longing turned to Wall street again. But before starting back he learned that some parties in Boston were desirous of buying the Bristol line of steamers, running on Long Island sound. It occurred to him that he might turn this circumstance to some account for himself, and this was the pretext for his next visit to New York. His first business was to secure a letter of introduction to the president of the company owning the coveted line of steamers. This he readily procured and presented. The person to whom he was thus introduced was the celebrated Daniel Drew. But for this meeting the world would probably never have heard of James Fisk, Jr. That event constitutes the most prominent and important landmark in his life, and turned his career into the course that has conducted him to his present position. The presidency of the Bristol Line Steamboat company was but one small bob on the Drew kite. Already past his three score and ten, he wore the scars of many fierce battles, some of which were still fresh and scarcely cicatriced. Born a farmer's boy, at Carmel, on the Harlem road, he had been successively a drover, proprietor of the Bull's Head tavern (of great fame in the olden time), and a large owner in steamboat enterprises. In this last character, he came into contact with Vanderbilt, and the two had since been lifelong rivals. He had been the Commodore's great antagonist in the then recent Harlem "corners"—the pioneer *coups de main* in Wall street stock jobbing operations, and in these had been badly worsted by his veteran foe. He was now the great Mogul of Erie—one of its directors, its treasurer, its sole manipulator, the first to use his position to gamble in the stock of his own corporation, already dubbed the "speculative director," and the acknowledged leader of Wall street's "bear" brigade. Drew was much pleased with his new acquaintance, was quite surprised and fascinated with the grand and liberal ideas which the young man very freely ventilated on the question of steamships and affairs generally, and immediately authorized him to act as his agent in negotiating the sale of the Bristol steamers. This trust was executed in a manner that confirmed and heightened the old gentleman's first impressions and gave him entire satisfaction, at the same time that it put a nice little sum into the skilful agent's pocket as his commission for conducting the transfer.

Mr. Fisk now looked upon Wall street as his headquarters again, but as he had learned that the game there was played with stocked cards and loaded dice he sagely concluded it would be much safer to have a finger in the stocking business or be privy to its manner, and make himself master of the magic cubes, instead of having them played on him again. He is not to he caught twice in the same trap. He had seen those "twenty-four jacks" fall out of Ah Sin's sleeves in the first hand of eucher and he was not going to sit down to the game again till he had a pair of sleeves just like Ah Sin's—only a little larger—and they should be well filled with right bowers. Drew, in the first flush of his admiration for the joung man's bearing, spoke the necessary words of encouragement, and shortly after the sign of a new firm of brokers appeared, bearing the firm name of Fisk & Belden. They made a specialty of dealing in Erie, and soon became known among the fraternity as Drew's brokers. The head of the firm being a special favorite, confidant and protege of the crafty director and treasurer, it is more than probable that he was privy to sufficient information and " points " not for general use, to enable him to operate on his own account with all desired safety and make much more than a simple commission as broker for others. It was in the spring of 1866 that Drew executed his first great master-stroke in qear operations, inaugurating a system of manipulations wholly original and unparalleled, making the entire bull clique writhe under his goad, and finally strewing the pavement with their skulls and bones, establishing for himself an enduring fame in the history and traditions of Wall streat. Fisk, being fully behind the scenes in this campaigne, enjoyed the sport immensely and turned his opportunity to much substantial account. He was immoderately amused at the mad boundings and bellowings of the rampant animals, shook a red flag before them to incite them on, and cried, " Habet! habet!" in delight as his uncle Dan'el poured in the final broadside and sent them reeling to the ground. This was an excellent school for the apt pupil. He took to its ways with a readiness that showed a genius for the science. The briefest period of tuition sufficed to make him master of its entire curriculum. All the scales having now fallen from his eyes, he resisted a longer pupilage and came forward at once as a professor. Having caught the principle and spirit of the process by which puppets were made to dance on the Wall street stage, he immediately saw that many improvements could be made in the *modus operandi* of his instructor, and felt he could play upon the magic keys much more deftly than he saw it done by the fingers clumsy in size and stiffened by the toils and chills of more than three score and ten winters. His subsequent career speaks for the close attention he paid during his brief term of schooling, and no one can testify better than the teacher how thoroughly the lesson was learned both in letter and spirit, for the pupil soon repaid the debt of gratitude, principal and interest, to his instructor by teaching him in turn many tricks at his own trade. But the improvements were of a nature requiring a cunning of hand which the veteran director could not hope to conjure in his weight of years, and it is more than doubtful if the instructor feels at all proud of his pupil, accurately as he has followed instructions and brilliant as his exploits flowing therefrom have been, for the teachings were returned in a practical way that was not highly appreciated, though its force was acknowledged. When the pupil had once seen how the cards were stacked, he brought to work such rare manual skill that he stocked them under his instructor's very eyes without his seeing it and playing them upon him before he was aware of it. After this had been repeated a few times, the old gentleman rose from the table, offended at this disrespect for his years and refused to play any more. He now stands a looker on at the table at which he was once master and, with hands folded behind him, he gazes with an expression of mute curiosity at the grace and dexterity with which his pupil shuffles the cards and throws the dice.

With wind and tide both in his favor, Mr. Fisk very soon recovered what he had involuntarily lent to Wall street, and it was but a few months before the man who had lost his last dollar, again had a bank account.

The last new episode in Mr. Fisk's career which caused his name to figure conspicuously in the papers for a few days, was of a totally different nature from all its predecessors, reading more like a chapter from Ixiom or Odyssey, while the others savored of the

Arabian Nights, and portraying that, through all his stern battling, and all the rude blasts that beat upon him, he had still preserved a tender and sensitive heart and strong affections, and that therein was his one vulnerable point—the one soft spot in the heel of Achilles.

In January last the footsteps of a young man were dogged about the city a great part of the night till he was finally caught and arrested on a charge of heavy embezzlements from the Brooklyn Oil Refining Co., of which he was secretary. The feature of the case developed rapidly. The young gent proved to have the kind of friends and influence that could unbolt his prison doors. He was soon restored to his full liberty, and it was then made to appear that his arrest had been instigated by James Fisk, Jr., that there was a modern Helen in the case, and that slighted love accounted for the milk in this cocoanut.

Miss Helen Josephine Mansfield, a beautiful B ston girl, went to California with her mother at sixteen, in 1854, to join her stepfather, there met and married the act r, Frank Lawlor the next year, lived with him about two years, when he obtained a divorce without opposition on her part, both being in New York at the time. She subsequently met Mr. Fisk, and he was greatly smitten with her at once and lavished upon her all the kindness and attention for which he was noted wherever his affections were enlisted. She lived on 23d street, near the Grand Opera House, in an elegant residence frescoed and furnished in the most luxuriant manner, sumptuously supplied with everything that Sybarite taste could desire or wealth procure. She had one of the grandest turnouts that was ever seen in the park, enjoyed the pleasures of Long Branch and was a conspicuous specimen of a certain type of beauty. There was no other place like Josie's for Mr. Fisk in the social hours. But this was one of those courses that proverbially never run smooth, and in time some disagreement sprung up in consequence of which Mr. Fisk received a note discontinuing the acquaintance and directing the removal of everything belonging to him in the house. This note naturally wounded the stout heart not a little, and was said to have affected him to tears.

Among the frequenters of Josie's elegant parlors was Edward S. Stokes, a fashionable young New Yorker, well acquainted with Mr. Fisk from business connection. On receiving the note that moved him so deeply. the Admiral took it to Mr. Stokes, and with tears in his eyes, as was reported, said, "See here, Ned, she won't even let me leave my gum shoes in the house!"

It was in vain that Mr. Stokes endeavored to make light of the matter and say all would come round right again. Mr. Fisk wanted him to discontinue visiting at Josie's, but this he would not consent to promise, and the Admiral retired with clouded brow. Soon Mr. Stokes was informed of the rescinding of certain verbal contracts for large amounts which he had with the Erie Railway. Next he was asked either to sell out his share in the Brooklyn Oil Refining Company, or buy out the other owners. He accepted the latter alternative and an agreement upon the price was fixed between him and Mr. Fisk, but the other owners would not assent to the arrangement made by Mr. Fisk, so it fell through. From these and other indications, Mr. Stokes knowing he had incurred the displeasure and enmity of Mr. Fisk, sent him a note asking for an interview at Delmonico's, that they might reconcile such an unworthy difference. The Admiral responded to the appointment, and on reaching the rendervous remarked to Mr. Stokes, " I thought I could cut nearer a man's heart than any one in New York, but you go plump through it." The interview promised little result, the one thing that would satisfy Mr. Fisk being just the one thing that the other would not consent to, and therefore Mr. Stokes proposed they sould leave it to Josie to decide between them. Mr. Fisk assented to the proposal. He had to drill with the Ninth that evening, and left the restaurant saying to Stokes, "Meet me in Josie's at half-past ten."

At the later interview the parties holding the same determination, Josie declined to decide between them, seeing no reason why they should not all be friends, neither concerning himself about the doings of the other. But Mr. Fisk was inexorable in the stand he had taken, and said, " It won't do, Josie ! You can't run two engines on one track in contrary directions at the same time." The interview was prolonged till the small hours of the night, and was said to have been attended with more tears, but at last ended without any change of the situation.

The next development in the matter was the arrest of Mr. Stokes on the charge of embezzlement, when all the facts as related came out in the papers. The charge was speedily dismissed as unsustained and the whole affair was quickly smothered, it proving to have stirred up a more than usually troublesome hornet's nest.

The next day after the above facts appeared in the papers, Mr. Fisk appeared in a characteristic letter to the *World* denying many of the statements, and reminding that paper of the "sacred mandate,"

"Thou shalt not bear false witness against thy neighbor." But the most amusing part of this letter was not in the body of the letter itself. It is said the most important part of a lady's letter is always in the postscript, and the remark is equally applicable to Mr. Fisk's letter in this instance. After quite a long statement of the facts and the appending of the sign manual, came:

"P. S. I only wish, where your article states I burst into tears that you gave the truth. Years ago, before the world battled me so fearfully, I have a vague recollection that emotions could be aroused which would call forth tears, but that is many years ago, far back before energy had taken such complete hold of us all, and before ambition swayed the minds of men as it now does. But the memory of those days is lasting, and I can recall that when night came a mother's hand was laid upon my head, and I was taught to repeat a simple prayer, and then I heard the words, 'My son, I must put you in your little bed.'
J. F., JR."

There is little need to say more concerning this fatal amour in this connection. Its subsequent progress and sad results are fully detailed in our other pages.

As there have been so many stories to of Colonel Fisk, and the part he played in the riot, a retail merchant on Eighth avenue, near Twenty-fifth street, makes this statement: "I sat in my second story window all through the firing; being on the west side, and seeing at a glance that the shots were mostly directed toward the east side, I did not shrink back. I saw Colonel Fisk there, in his shirt sleeves, several minutes before the heavy fusilade. I can testify that none of the crowd of rioters came near him. When the shots came thick, the crowd mainly rushed for the houses on the east. When Wyatt and Page fell, their comrads fired mostly toward the southwest corner of Twenty-fifth street and up that street. Then they recoiled in confusion toward my side of the street, bringing Fisk with them. Some of them dropped down a moment, with the idea, apparently, of giving the Seventh, who were on this side, a chance to fire over their heads. One company, close by me, behaved pretty well, but they neglected to reload. It seemed to me that a hundred resolute rioters coming from the other side at that moment could have swept off the whole of them. I was so excited at their not loading that I scarcely knew what I did, and jumped out on the cornice and yelled at them, 'Why don't you load? Why don't you load?' Some of them did so, but I tell you the rioters disappeared quick. In a few moments the street was as quiet as a church-yard. The soldiers who did not march on with the rest got into the houses. I went into Parker's, and saw Fisk lying on his back on a bed in the second story with his arms stretched out, looking like a great fat turtle. To my thinking he showed the white feather all through. He seemed quite taken up with the idea of his own safety, and was all the while imagining there was a great crowd after him. He said to me, 'I suppose the sooner I get away from here the quicker the crowd will get away." I told him there was no crowd before the house, and not a dozen people. I told him I would get a carriage to take him. He looked toward the back yard, and asked if he could not get over that way. Parker said: "You will have to get over the fence." Fisk said: "I can do that." So he hobbled out. They put a short step-ladder on Parker's side of the fence, and he wobbled up on top. You should have seen him, sitting astride that fence while they passed the steps over. He looked this way and that way, and then got into the yard on the other side. The house there is occupied by a Hessian family, who disguised him, and kept him there a good while. After about fifteen minutes he came out on the back stoop to look around, and that was the last I saw of him. I know it was there he was disguised, because the little boys of that family said to my little boys, " You ought to see how father fixed up Col. Fisk. He blacked his moustache, and put an old overcoat on him, and made him look like an old man." My impression at the time was that he had no confidence in himself as a military leader. I think, now, that he was scared nearly to death."

The Hessian family turns out to be that of an Irishman named Hession, who thus deposes:

"I was out in the street when the firing began. I was not frightened at all. I only just made up my mind that I would save some poor creature's life, and I did. I saved several. But you want to know about Colonel Fisk. I know more than I can tell now; but it will all come out. That man would have been all in inch pieces if it had not been for me. I would do the same for any poor creature, but I saved his life, anyhow. I helped him down from the fence, and took him in at the price of my own life. If the rioters had known at the time that I, an Irishman, did this, they would have torn me in pieces. I got him in, and blacked his mustache, and got him a pair of my pantaloons. You ought to have seen him getting into them. I'm a small man, you know, and it was a tight squeeze. I wanted to rip them some, but he would not let me. I had no coat big enough for him, so I gave him an old overcoat, and the worst hat in the house. He was the worst scared man you ever saw. He's no business to be a Colonel. He kept getting scared about the mob coming for him, and for me. I was not frightened a bit. I went out in the street, and walked about and told him, 'Look at me, I ain't frightened, and you needn't be.' One time he went on top of the house, but I made him come down. He must have stayed three hours, and there were other soldiers here. Its all nonsense about his going to Twenty-seventh street and the rest of those streets across lots and over fences. He walked away from here to Ninth avenue, where he took a carriage that was waiting for him."

HELEN JOSEPHINE MANSFIELD.

LIFE OF
HELEN JOSEPHINE MANSFIELD,
THE "PRINCESS OF ERIE."

CHAPTER I.

SKETCH OF THE LIFE OF MISS MANSFIELD. HER BIRTH-PLACE—HER MOTHER—HER OWN MARRIAGE—SEPARATION FROM HER HUSBAND—FIRST ACQAINTANCE WITH COL. FISK—INTRODUCTION TO STOKES—COL. FISK'S LETTERS, ETC., ETC.

Mrs. or Miss Helen Josephine Mansfield was born in Boston, in the year of 1848—consequently her age is 24. While she was yet a child her father died, and her mother was left in comparative poverty, and but for the kindness of a brother of her deceased husband, would have been compelled to face the world and fight the hard battles of life to win for herself and her child their bread. To his elegant home they were invited, and in that abode of luxury and refinement they were made honored guests. Mr. Mansfield was a batchelor, and his household was under the supervision of a housekeeper who had been for some years in charge, and who still remained after the arrival of the young widow and her winsome little daughter. It is said of the lady that she was exceeding fair to look upon and her presence in that stately house was the first ray of sunshine that had lit up its gloom for many years. I have said that Mr. Mansfield was unmarried and away back in his early life, was a romance—in what life is there not—and a vision of a beautiful woman who had won his heart, toyed with it while it amused her, then cast it aside, mocking as it lay broken and quivering at her feet, haunted his waking and sleeping hours. I suppose he accepted his fate as many another has done, and gathered up the broken fragments of the hopes that had been woven with threads as bright as if dyed in tropical rainbows, and folded them away in some secret recess of his heart, looking sometimes at the face of the dead love only to be sure that it had no life —laying his hand softly on its still bosom to be sure it never throbbed with even the lightest movement under its shroud. The influence of a young and beautiful woman could but be felt in such a home, and he thought it would be a joy forever to see her at his hearth and in his halls, as mistress of the home that drew all its brightness from her.

The lady listened, toying suggestively with the deep folds of crape upon her bombazine, but though the long lashes drooped upon her round, fair cheek, there is little doubt but " there was speculation in her eye," and it is on record that when her year of mourning had expired, she exchanged her sable robes for snowy satin, or sheeny silk, and her dismal weeds for orange flowers and illusion. It is further recorded that for a few brief bright days the devoted lover husband found her " all his fancy painted her," but as the days stretched out into months, there came a change over the spirit of his dreams and he woke to the consciousness of the bitter fact that he was but the tool by which she gratified her ambitious love of dress and display. He was a quiet, unostentatious man—she was a proud vain, showy woman. He was fond of quiet and retirement, she was, eager for excitement and stimulant. He was thoughtful and studious, she shallow and superficial. No one need be told that for each the marriage was a wrong step, and that only misery could be the result. Very soon her course took its first downward step. She dressed richly and gaily for the street, the promenade, or the various places of amusement she frequented, some of them of more than doubtful character, and filled her house with men whom no pure woman would tolerate in her presence—then there were stolen interviews and secret appointments stealthily kept, then society busied itself with her name and soon rumors came to the husband's ears of the guilty intrigues with which his wife was connected. At first he was incredulous. Had thunderbolts fallen at his feet from the cloudless June sky above him, or the walls rattled in ruins around him, it would not have astonished him more. A few days of quiet observation, a few direct questions put judiciously to the servants and the horrible suspicions became more horrible certainties. For a while the power of action seemed denied him, and he was paralyzed by the blow—then the keen sense of disgrace and dishonor stung the man to the heart. That it should have come upon him in *any* form would have been bad enough—that it had come upon him in *this* form, made the disgrace seem doubly disgraceful and the dishonor doubly dishonorable. To have been compelled to receive it at the hand of his most merciless foe, would have been sufficiently humiliating, but to have it forced upon him by the hand of the wife whom he loved almost to worship, was unendurable. The time when men washed out their wrongs in the life blood of another, at the bidding of the worlds "code of honor," had passed by, and the law was sufficiently strong to deal out justice to the offender. To that law he appealed, and its verdict was that what *man* had joined together, *man* could put assunder, and accordingly a decree of divorce was issued, and henceforth their paths lay severed far and wide, never to mingle in one channel again. Her next adventures were in the far west, and we learn that where the bright waves of the Pacific wash over sands of gold, she spread her nets, and became a "fisher of men," in the service of the prince of darkness. What wonder that under such tuition the little Josie learned lessons which she remembered only too well, and carried into effect in later years. Of her marriage with the young actor, Frank Lawlor,—of their wretched domestic life, and its short duration, all the world knows. Upon her reappearance in the east, it is said that her course of infamy was so open and unblushing, so disgustingly defiant of law and order and the opinions of the world, that at one time, in Philadelphia, she was threatened with violence at the hands of the outraged community, and the beautiful Cyprian prudently withdrew to New York, judging correctly that in a city noted for the laxity of its moral principles, it would be for her to choose her own course and her own victims. It was at this time that she met James Fisk, Jr., and that he fell an easy prey to her arts is not strange. No ancient Helen was so radiant in her beauty as her modern namesake. Fisk was an infatuated lover. Fortune, fame, honor, every thing but his name lay at her feet, and this velvet lipped Delilah never hesitated to deliver him, shorn of his strength, into the hands of the Philistines. If the boldness and open defiance of public opinion which characterized the whole affair were to be commented upon, the world's verdict would be summed up in one word, "shameless." Her attempt to support herself as an actress was a failure, and disgusted and desperate, she turned like a wild beast at bay and declared, in the face of morality and decency that "if her talents would not support her, her beauty should;" and in order that her stock in trade might bring her its highest market value, she laid siege to the citadel of Colonel Fisk's heart and purse. How fully and freely each were surrendered, we all know, and the world wonders at the magnificent prodigality with which he lavished a princely fortune upon her. That she repaid his love with selfishness is only what might have been expected of her. It is told of Cleopatria that she tore from her arms and bosom the pearls with which they were decked, each one of which would have been a fit ransom for a king, and dissolving them in vinegar in her goblet, drank them to the health of her royal lover, Mark Antony, but *this* Cleopatra, some sentimental writer who had not a very nice regard for truth, asserts in defiance of established facts, that she sacrificed honor, virtue, position, everything for him, when it is well known that no pearl of great price had she to give. As long ago as 1868 or 1869, Fisk purchased her a house and assumed the entire responsibility of defraying her expenses, no very light thing, and from that time until the day of his death, she was entirely dependent upon him. That Col. Fisk was affectionate and confiding in his disposition, is proven by the manner in which he introduced to her his dearest friend, Edward Stokes, encouraging their acquaintance, with a trust in their honor which should have saved him from the betrayal and wrong received at their hand. His love for Stokes was something wonderful—tender and blind as a woman, and not until he was forced to would he believe that they had wronged him. A constant correspondence was kept up, even though they met almost daily. We give, so far as they have been published, the letters from Fisk to Miss Mansfield. They speak a sincere affection which we can but regret was not bestowed upon a more worthy object.

The letters commence by a note written by Fisk when Josie lived in Lexington avenue, on his visiting card, as follows·

Mrs. JOSIE LAWLOR, 42 Lexington avenue:

Come. Will you come over with Fred and dine with me? If your friends are there bring them along. Yours, truly, J. F., JR.

Have not heard from you as you promised.

On the back of the card was the following:

Come. Fred is at the door. My room, eight o'clock. After many good looks I found Mr. Chamberlain. The understanding is now that yourself and Miss Land are to go with me, say at half-past nine o'clock, and the above gentleman is to come at eleven o'clock, as he has some matters to attend to which will take him until that time. Answer this, if you will be ready by half-past nine o'clock. Yours, truly. JAMES FISK, JR.

JOSIE SPREADS HERSELF.

After Fisk began to furnish Josie with money, away back in 1868, she began to ride out in great style. One day she came into the Opera House in magnificent apparel, to the astonishment of the employes.

The next day Fisk wrote the following scolding note on his visiting card:

Strange you should make my office or the vicinity the scene for a "personal." You must be aware that harm came to me in such foolish vanity, and those that could do it care but little for the interest of the writer of this. Yours, truly, JAMES FISK, JR.

In January, 1868, Fisk seemed to be in a Picwickian mood, for he came the "chops and tomato sauce" in the following laconic:

5TH AVE. H.

DOLLY—Enclosed find money. Bully morning for a funeral!

J. F., JR.

Here comes a fishy despatch, characteristic of the Colonel:

DEAR JOSIE—Get ready and come to the Twenty-third street entrance of the hotel and take me down town, and then you can come back and get the girls for the Fulton dinner to-day.

Yours, truly, SARDINES.

It seems Josie was going off on a journey, and Fisk provides for her like a devoted lover:

DOLLY—The baggage sleigh will call at one o'clock, and you can leave in my charge what you see fit. You have no time to lose.

J. F., JR.

Then comes a sober note from J. Fisk, through J. C. (John Corner), Fisk's private secretary:

MRS. MANSFIELD—The sleigh will call for you at two P. M.

Yours, J. FISK, per J. C.

Here comes a quiet note, as if written by the head of a family; but it is full of devotion. It is the first regularly-dated note presented:

My people are partaking of New York, in the shape of "White Fawn," and two or three other different matters. I may not be able to see you again to-night. If not, will take breakfast with you—the best I could do. Yours, truly,

February 5, 1868. JAMES.

So we see how Fisk kept his word, for he sent a boy off to "Josie" with this note in the morning:

DEAR DOLLY—Get right up now and I will be down to take breakfast with you in about thirty minutes. We will take breakfast in the main dining room down stairs. Yours, truly,
Wednesday Morning, February 6. JAMES FISK, JR.

To-day Fisk sent " Dolly " some money, saying:
Have the kindness to acknowledge. Yours truly,
February, 22, 1868. J. F., jr.

To-night Fisk went to the opera with Josie.

DEAR JOSIE—I have got some matters to arrange and cannot call for you until it is about time to go. I will be there twenty minutes before eight. Be ready. Yours truly, JAMES.
February 26, 1868

SLEEP, DOLLY, SLEEP!

What a sweet, pretty note is this! Who wouldn't sleep well with a sweet note from the Prince of Erie, and a present of $50?

DOLLY—Enclosed find $50 Sleep, Dolly, all the sleep you can to-day—every little bit! Sleep, Dolly! I feel as if three cents' worth of clams would help me some. Yours, truly, J. F. JR.

What filial love is displayed in this note! Oh! Josie! Fisk loved his wife the best after all!

Monday Morning.

I am going to the San Francisco Minstrels with my family. If Mr. L. was here I should ask him to take you. Shall see you to-morrow evening. Yours, truly, J. F., JR.

But what a nice compensation—to send money when he could not come himself! That ought to satisfy any one:

DOLLY—Enclosed find———. I am wrong, but am bothered. I will come right. When I don't come don't wait. You shall not be placed as you were to-night. Yours, truly,
Wed. Evening. JAMES FISK, JR.
Have the kindness to acknowledge. Yours truly,
Feb. 22, 1868. J. F., JR.

TWEED AND SIR MORTON PETO.

Now we come to affairs of State. It is to be hoped that Tweed and Sir Morton had a good dinner, and that Dolly looked lovely:

187 West Street, Tuesday, October 13, 1868.

MY DEAR JOSIE—James McHenry, the partner of Sir Morton Peto, the largest railway builder in the world, Mr. Tweed and Mr. Lane, will dine with us at half-past six o'clock. I want you to provide as nice a dinner as possible. Everything went off elegantly. We are *all* safe. Will see you at six o'clock.   JAMES FISK, JR.

HONEYMOON PASSED.

Josie and James now began to be so intimate that few letters were written, and these were of a solid and substantial kind, almost always containing money. As we give every letter mentioned in the affidavits, of course these slip in with the rest:

Monday, Aug. 2, 1869.

DEAR JOSIE—Send my valise, with two shirts, good collars, vest, handkerchiefs, black velvet coat, nice vest, patent leather shoes, light pants. I am going to Long Branch to see about the calerye. Inclosed find $25. Be back in the morning.   J. F., JR.

What a generous man was Fisk! To-day he sends more money:

St. James Hotel, Sunday, Oct. 18, 1869.

DEAR JOSIE—Inclosed you will find $143. Yours, truly,
JAMES.

A LITTLE TROUBLE.

Fisk had been having a little scold with Josie about this time. Josie wanted Fisk to make a settlement on her, and Fisk wouldn't. But Fisk's forgiving disposition is here illustrated:

February 10, 1869.

MY DEAR DOLLY—Will you see me this morning? If so, what hour? Yours truly, ever,   JAMES.

How like a good husband did Fisk notify Dolly of his comings and goings? If every married man in New York was as kind as Fisk was to his "Dolly," how happy the world would be! Here comes a telegram from Worcester, Mass.:

[Western Union Telegraph Company.]

WORCESTER, Mass.

[Received at Thirtieth street, February 14, 1870.]
To H. J. Mansfield, 350 West Twenty-third street.

On the three o'clock train from Boston. Shall be in New York at twelve.   (13 D. H.)   J. F., JR.

What a nice apology for not coming to dinner is here sent! Generous Fisk!

10th of March.

DEAR DOLLY—Inclosed find $75, which you need; do not wait dinner for me to-night; I cannot come. Yours truly, ever,

JAMES.

A LOVE QUARREL.

Josie seemed now enthroned in Fisk's affections. That he loved her was plain to all. But this did not satisfy her. She saw her charms slowly fading, and, though she had a present competency, who was to take care of her in the far future? What if, by and by, Fisk should tire of her?

On the 28th of January, 1870, Josie declared she would leave Fisk if he didn't make over to her a competency for life. Fisk refused. The next day Josie wrote him a threatening letter, saying their relations were ended. Fisk received it with sorrow, and then replied:

SUNDAY EVENING, Feb. 1, 1870.

MY DEAR JOSIE—I received your letter. The tenor does not surprise me much. You alone sought the issue, and the reward will belong to you. I cannot allow you to depart believing yourself what you write, and must say to you, which you know full well, that all the differences could have been settled by a kiss in the right spirits, and in after days I should feel very kindly toward you out of memory of the great love I have borne for you. I never was aware that you admitted a fault. I have many—God knows, too many—and that has brought me the trouble of the day. I will not speak of the future, for full well I know the spirits you take it in. "You know me," and the instincts of your heart will weigh me out in the right scale. I will give you no parting advice. You have been well schooled in that, and can tell chaff from wheat, and probably are as strong to-night as the humble writer of this letter. The *actions* of the past *must* be the right way to think of me; and from them, day by day, I hope any comparison which you may make from writing in the future will be favorable for me. A longer letter from me might be much of an advertisement of my weakness, and the only great idea I would impress on your mind, is how wrong you are when you say that I have "grown tired of you." Wrong, wrong! Never excuse yourself on that in after years. Don't try to teach your heart that, for it is a lie, and you are falsifying yourself to your own soul.

No more. Like the Arabs, we will fold our tents and quietly steal away, and when we spread them next we hope it will be where the "woodbine twineth," over the river Jordan, on the bright and beautiful banks of heaven.　　From yours, ever.　　JAMES.

TOGETHER AGAIN.

In a few days after, Fisk wrote the last letter "Josie" sent for him; then she went to see him, and soon the trouble was all made up again. Four months afterwards we find Fisk enclosing her money and sending such letters as these:

MY DEAR JOSIE—Enclosed find your request. I will send to the Fifth Avenue for the things. I cannot go to the house, as much as I would like to.　　Yours,　　JAMES.
MAY 6, 1870.

COMPTROLLER'S OFFICE, ERIE RAILWAY COMPANY,
NEW YORK, MAY, 1870.

DOLLY—What do you think of this man? I told him you would talk to him, and then tell him to come back to me next Monday, and I will talk to you about it. Yours, ever,　　JAMES.

Who the above man was we do not know.

Now comes in seemingly irrelevant matter. Who John S. Williams is we do not know, and W Wilkins is a mystery to us; but, perhaps Stokes knew what it meant when he put the telegrams with the other letters:

ERIE RAILROAD TELEGRAPH, NEW YORK, April 20, 1870.
[From Chicago, Ill.]

To JAS. FISK, JR.:

John S. Williams, colored, is here without tickets or money. He has letters from our agent at San Francisco. Mr. A. J. Day; E. S. Spencer, at Omaha. Advise me what to do. He wants to leave on (4:45) to-morrow.　　A. J. DAY.
　　per A. M. McGeddis, Ticket Agent.
(Answered Sheridan.)

ERIE RAILROAD TELEGRAPH, NEW YORK, April 26, 1870.
To A. J. DAY, Chicago:

Yes. Send John S. Williams through on my account.
(9—)
[Written in lead pencil by J. F., Jr.]

W. Wilkins should be here in thirty hours from Chicago, when he will be directed to your house.　　Yours, truly,　　J. F., Jr.

THE BIG DIAMOND PIN.

It seems that Fisk trusted his $18,000 diamond pin with Josie, for he thus affectionately sends for it:

C. OFFICE, May 31, 1870.

Please send me the diamond brooch and necklace, my dear.

JAMES.

A COLDNESS.

It seems that Fisk began to grow cold about this time. Montaland had arrived from Paris, and the Prince of Erie was paying court to her. It was all fair—Josie had Stokes, and Fisk had Montaland. This letter is full of heartfelt regret:

AUGUST 1, 1870.

MY DEAR JOSIE—I send you letter I found to my care on my desk. I cannot come to you to-night. I shall stay in town to-night, and probably, to-morrow night, and after that I must go East. On my return I shall come to see you. I am sure you will say, "What a fool!" But you must rest and so must I. The thread is so slender I dare not strain it more. I am sore, but God made me so, and I have not the power to change it.

Loving you, as *none but you*, I am, yours ever. JAMES.

STOKES AND A PLOTTING HOUSE.

In the quarrel between Josie and Fisk, Miss Nully Pieris, Mr. Rane and Stokes seem to have been suspected by Fisk of plotting against him. He thus complains of a despatch which "Rane" sent to Stokes, who was at Saratoga or Buffalo, to come to New York:

August 4, 1870.

DEAR JOSIE—I found on my arrival at my office that the following dispatch had passed West last night:

F. S. Stokes, Buffalo and Saratoga Springs:

Pay no attention to former dispatch. Come on first train.

RANE.

Of course *it means* nothing that *you are aware of*. But let me give you the author of it and my authority, and you will see how faithfully they have worked the case out after my departure last evening. Miss Pieris drove directly to Rane's office; from there to the corner of Twenty-second street and Broadway, where the above dispatch was sent, and from there to Rulley's. A third party was with them, but who left them there? "Rane and Pieris, why should they heed Stokes?" "Comment is unnecessary"—a plotting house and against me. What have "I done" that Nully Pieris should work against my peace of mind. Yours truly, ever,

JAMES.

P. S.—Since writing the within, I understand, a dispatch has reached New York that he is on his way. JAMES.

JOSIE DESERTS FISK.

Josie now deserted Fisk because he would not give her a life competency, and linked her destinies with Stokes. Notwithstanding, Fisk pays bills and generously furnishes Josie with money.

August 14, 1870.

Enclosed you will find $400 for your little matters. You told me when I saw you last you would send me your bills, which I would be pleased to receive, and they shall have my attention at once. Your letter would require a little time to prepare a right answer to, so I will answer it more fully by to-morrow, when I can look at it more carefully over. I am very happy to know that you have acted from no impulse in leaving me, but that it was a long matured plan. I hope you have made no mistake. Yours truly, ever,

JAMES FISK, JR.

JOSIE WRITES TO FISK.

This is the letter which Josie wrote to Fisk, and which he desired to take time to reply to. In this letter Josie says she has never received a dollar from any one but Fisk, It is Josie's last letter:
JAMES FISK, JR.:

That your letter had the desired effect you can well imagine. I am honest enough to admit it cut me to the quick. In all the annals of letter writing I may say it eclipsed them all. Your secretary made a slight error, however, in supposing that Mlle. Montaland was mentioned. The only prima donna I referred to was " Miss Pieris." As you say, Mlle. has nothing whatever to do with my affairs. I have always respected her, and only thought of her as one of the noblest works of God—beautiful and talented and *your choice*—never referring to her in my letter in thought or word. I freely admit that I never expected so severe a letter from you. I, of course, feel that it was unmerited, but, as it is your opinion of me, I accept it with all the sting. You have *struck home*, and, I may say, turn the knife around. I will send you the picture you speak of at once. The one in the parlor I will also dispose of. I know of nothing else here that you would wish. I am anxious to adjust our affairs. I certainly do not wish to annoy you, and that I may be able to do so I write you this last letter. You have told me very often that you held some twenty or twenty-five thousand dollars of mine in your keeping. I do not know if it is so, but that I may be able to shape my affairs permanently for the future that a part of the amount would place me in a position where I never would have to appeal to you for aught. I have never *had one dollar from any one else*, and arriving here from the Branch, expecting my affairs with you to continue, I contracted bills that I would not otherwise have done. I do not ask for anything I have not been led to suppose was mine, and do not ask you to settle what is not entirely convenient for you. After a time I shall sell my house, but for the present think it best to remain in it. The money I speak of would place me where I should not need the assistance of no one.

The ring I take back as fairly as I gave it you; the mate to it I shall keep for company. Why you should say I obtained this house by robbery I cannot imagine; however, you know best. I am sorry that your associations with me was detrimental to you, and I would gladly, with you (were it possible), obliterate the last three year's of my life's history; but it is not possible, and we must struggle to outlive our past. I trust you will take the sense of this letter as it is meant, and that there can be no mistake I send this by Ella, and what you do not undetstand she will explain.

FISK TO JOSIE.

To this and other letters of Josie, Fisk made the following reply :

NEW YORK, Oct. 1, 1870.

Mrs. Mansfield—There can be no question as to the authority of the letter which was handed to me yesterday by your servant, in this respect differing from the epistle which you say you receive from Miss Pieris, and which, in your opinion required the united efforts of herself, Mlle. Montaland and myself. Certainly the composition should be good if these two parties had combined to produce it. But the slight mistake you make is evident from the fact that the letter referred to was never seen by me, and I presume Mlle. Montaland is equally ignorant of its existence, as it is not likely she troubled herself about your affairs. I can scarcely believe that she assisted Miss Pieris in composing the letter, and the credit is therefore due to Miss Pieris for superior talent in correspondence. As far as the great exposure you speak of is concerned, that is a dark story upon which I have no light, and as I fail to see it I cannot, of course, understand it. I have endeavored to put your jumbled letter together in order to arrive at your meaning, and I presume I have some idea of what you wish to convey; but as your statements lack the important element of truth they cannot, of course, have any weight with me. You may not be to blame for entertaining the idea that you have shown great kindness to Miss Pieris, and others, and that they are under great obligations to you for favors conferred. The habit of constantly imagining that you were the real author of all the benefits bestowed upon others would naturally affect a much better balanced brain than yours, and in time you would come to believe that you alone had the power to distribute the good things to those around you, utterly forgetful of him who was behind the scenes utterly unnoticed.

Can you blame, then, those from whose eyes the evil has fallen, and who see you in your true light as the giver of other's charities? I would not trouble myself to answer your letters, and I do not consider it a duty I owe you to give you a final expression of my opinion. In venting your spite on Miss Pieris (with whose affairs, by the way, I have nothing whatever to do) you have written a letter, in answering which you afforded me an opportunity of conveying to you my ideas respecting the theories which you have taken every opportunity to express to those around you, and which many people have considered merely the emanations of a crazy brain. I could not coincide with this view, for crazy people are not inclined to do precisely as they please either right or wrong, and so long as they are *loose* I consider them sane, and therefore I could not put that construction on your conversation. As for Miss Pieris being "a snake in the grass," I care but little about that. She can do me neither harm nor good. I have done all that has been done for her during the past year. She comes to me and says: "Sir, you have been my friend; you have assisted me in my troubles, and I thank you from the bottom of my heart." That is a full and sufficient recompense for me, for any good I may have done her, and she can return. If she be a snake in the grass, I know full well her sting is gone and she is harmless. But what think you of a woman who would veil my eyes first by a gentle kiss, and afterward, night and day, for weeks, months and years, by deceit and fraud, to lead me through the dark valley of trouble, when she could have made my path one of roses, committing crimes which a devil incarnate would shrink from, while all this time I showed to her, as to you, nothing but kindness, both in words and actions, laying at your feet a soul, a heart, a fortune and a reputation which had cost by night and day twenty-five years of perpetual struggle, and which, but for the black blot of having in an evil hour linked itself with you, would stand out to-day brighter than any ever seen upon earth. But the mist has fallen, and you appear in your true light. I borrow your own words to describe you, "a snake in the grass," and verily, I have found thee out; and you have the audacity to call your sainted mother to witness your advice to me. "A dog that bites," etc.

You accuse her of leading you on and of ever standing ready to make appointments for you. The tone of your letter is such that you seem willing to shoulder the load of guilt under which an ordinary criminal would stagger. I believe you have arrived at that state when no amount of guilt will disturb your serenity or prevent your having sweet dreams, and we still shall see you crawl "a snake in the grass."

How I worship the night. I said, "Get thee behind me, Satan!" The few weeks that have elapsed since that blessed hour, how I bless them for the peace of mind they have brought me! Again the world looks bright, and I have a being. You imagined I would pursue you again, and you thought I would endeavor to tear down the castle you had obtained by robbery. God knows that if I am an element so lost to every feeling of decency as to be willing to link itself with you, I will assist and foster it, so that it will keep you from crawling towards me and prevent me from looking on you as a snake, as you are, and from raising a hand in pity to assist you should trouble again cross your path. So I have no fears that I will again come near you. I send you back a ring; and, were I to write anything about it, the words would be only too decent for the same, were they couched in the worst of language. So I say, take it back. Its memory is indecent, and it is the last souvenir I have that reminds me of you. I had a few pictures of you, but they have found a place among the nothings which fill the waste basket under my table. I am aware that in your back parlor hangs the picture of the man who gave you the wall to hang it on; and rumor says you have another in your chamber. The picture up stairs send back to me. Take the other down, for he whom it represents has no respect for you. After you read this letter, you should be ashamed to look at the picture, for you would say, "With all thy faults I love thee still," and what would be merely the same oft-repeated *lie*. So take it down. Do not keep anything in that house that looks like me.

If there are any unsettled business matters that it is proper for me to arrange, send them to me, and make the explanation as brief as possible.

I fain would reach the point where not even the slightest necessity will exist for any intercourse between us. I am in hopes this will end it.

JAMES FISK, JR.

FISK TO JOSIE AGAIN.

On the 4th of October Fisk wrote to Josie again, relative to the $25,000 which she wanted from him. He also mentioned Stokes as the weak element, &c. "Etta" is Mrs. Williams:—

NEW YORK, Oct. 4, 1870.

After the departure of Etta to-day I wasted time enough to read over once more the letter of which she was the bearer from you to me, and I determined to reply to it, for the reason that if it remained unanswered, you might possibly think I did not really mean what I said when I wrote; and besides, I was apprehensive that the friendly talk carried on through Etta, at second hand, between you and me, might lead you to suppose I had somewhat repented of the course I had taken, or of the words I had penned. It is to remove any such impression that I again write to you, as I would have the language of my former letter and the sentiments therein expressed stamped upon your heart as my deep-seated opinion of your character. No other construction must be put up upon my words. I turn over the first page of your letter; I pass over the kind words you have written; have I not furnished a satisfactory mansion for others' use? Have I not fulfilled every promise I have made? Is there not a stability about your finances to-day (it not disturbed by vultures) sufficient to afford you a comfortable income for the remainder of your natural life? You say you have never received a dollar from any one but me, and you *will never* have another from me, until want and misery bring you to my door, except, of course, in fulfillment of my sacred promise, and the settlement of your bills up to three weeks ago, at five minutes to eleven o'clock.

You need not have any fear as to my sensitiveness regarding your calling on any one else for assistance, as I find the word "*assistance*" underlined in your letter to make it the more impressive on my mind. That of all others is the point I would have you reach; for in that you would say, "Why man, how beautiful you are to look at, but nothing to lean on!" And you may well imagine my surprise at the selection of the element you have chosen to fill my place (Stokes). I was shown to-day his diamonds, which had been sacrificed to our people at one-half their value, and undoubtedly if this were not so the money would have been turned over to you, that you might feel contented as to the permanency of your affairs. You will therefore excuse me if I decline your modest request for a still further disbursement of $25,000. I very naturally feel that some part of this amount might be used to release from the pound the property of others in whose welfare the writer of this does *not* feel unbounded interest.

You say that you hope I will make sense of your letter. There is but one sense to be taken out of it, and that is an "epitaph," to be cut on the stone at the head of the grave in which Mrs. Helen Josephine Mansfield has buried her pride. Had she been the same proud-spirited girl that she was when she stood side by side with me—the power behind the throne—she would not have humbled herself to ask a permanency of one whom she had so deeply wronged, nor would she stoop to be indebted to him for a home which would have furnished a haven of rest, pleasure and debauchery without cost to those who had crossed his path and robbed him of the friendship he once felt. The length of time since I had her and the kind words she spoke, left my mind ill prepared for the perusal of your letter at that time, and it was not until after her departure, when I was seated quietly alone, that I took in the full intent and meaning of your letter, and felt that it was "robbery," and nothing else. Now, pin this letter with the other. The front of this is the back of that, and you will have a telescopic view of yourself and your character, as you appear to me to-day; and then I ask you to turn back from pages of your life's history, counting each page one week of your life, and see how I looked to thee then, and ask your own guilty heart if you had not better let me alone; and instead of trying to answer this letter from your disorganized brain, or writing from the dictation of those around you to-day, simply take a piece of paper and write on it the same as I do now, so far as we are now, or ever may be, "Dust to dust, ashes to ashes. Amen." J. F., Jr.

A little difference of opinion arose as to bills. Fisk maintained that after Josie left him and went with Stokes, that Stokes ought to pay the bills, and Fisk thus writes to Josie:

(J. F., Jr.) [Monogram.]

Oct. 19, 1870.

MADAME—Enclosed I send you bill of Harris receipted, and I also beg to hand you $126.29, being the honest proportion of the Bassford bill which belongs to me to pay. I should have made the word "honest" more definite, for had not Mr. Bassford to put the dates to the bill, as he had received instructions from Miss Mansfield, to have the bill all under the date of June 8, 1870, although (146.26) the amount of the goods, as bought by you or your agent, was spent at a much later date. I should not suppose you would care to place yourself in the light that this bill puts you, knowing as I do the instructions that you gave Mr. Bassford. I had supposed you "honest," but I find that a trace of that virtue does not even cling to you.

I am, yours, J. F., JR.

FISK'S LOVE FOR JOSIE.

Fisk's love for Josie at one time amounted to worship. It was hard for him to kill it, and day after day he used to spend writing to her. Here is another letter similar to the last :.

DEPARTMENT OF FINANCE,
New York, Oct. 20, 1870.

MADAM.—You know I would not wrong you, and I would take back all my acts when there could be a shadow of doubt that you was right and I was wrong; and let me speak of the other harsh letters I have written. I wrote them because you had wronged me positively, because you had placed between me and my life, my hope and my happiness an eternal gulf, and I felt sore and revengeful, and on those letters I am now the same. It would be idle for me to write aught about them or about *us*, when I could talk to you there. You did not listen. I presume it to be the same now. The entire connection is like a dream to me, a fearful dream, from which I have awoke, and, while dreaming, supposed my soul had gone out, and the awakening tells me I am saved, and from the embers of the late fire, there smoulders no spirit of revenge towards you, for you acted right, and the *wrong* only came to me from you because you did not act sooner, and I would not believe that any power on earth would make any question of money influence me or come between me and the holy feeling I once had for you. I sent John to Bassford's and they told him what I said, or he told me so, that you left word that the dates of the bill should not be changed. But what does it matter whether it is so or not? I cannot *feel* that you would do it, and something says to me, this was one of the things she was not like. So I pass it by, and if the letters of last night or to-day are not like me you can wash the bad act out from your memory and leave but the one idea that I want to do my duty and fulfill every unsettled relic. At least in my heart rests no remorse, for the memory is too deeply seated, and I would cherish all that is good about you, and forget forever the bad. Of late you have thought different from me (this may be imaginary on my part), for which I think you give me all the credit you can. We have *parted forever*. Now, let us make the memory of the past as bright and beautiful as we can, for on my side there is so little to cherish that I cling to it with great tenacity, and hope from time to time to wear it off. You *know* full well how I have suffered. *Once* you knew me better than any one on earth. To-day you know *me less*. It is the proper light for you to stand in. It is *all* you deserve on your desire. It is all you deserve *on mine*.

This letter should remain and be read only by you. Should you see fit to answer it, the answer will be the same way kept by me. There has been a storm. The ship, a noble steamer, has gone down. The storm is over and the sea is smooth again.

> Little ships should keep near shore,
> Greater ships can venture more.

"My ship is small and poorly officered."
I am yours, ever, etc., etc.,   J. F. JR.

P. S.—I would have liked to have answered your letter in full, but, as you say I have not a well-balanced brain, and I know I could not do justice to a letter of that kind, so refrain, and content to let the sentiments of it "know and fret me."

Josie used to call on Fisk frequently during the month of October. She frequently importuned him for money. Sometimes Fisk would see her, and this would unnerve him. As much as he had resolved on separation, her presence always melted his heart. This letter explains itself:

OCTOBER 25, 1870.

Why should I write to you again? Shall I ever reach the end? There comes another and another chapter, until I get weary with the entire affair. I would forget it and no doubt you would the same. The mistake yesterday was almost the mistake of a life-time for me.

MRS. MANSFIELD'S HOUSE, 359 23d. St, N. Y.

Who supposed for an instant that you would ever cross my path again in a spirit of submission and a contrite spirit? You have done that you should be sorry for, and I see the same in permitting it. This cannot be, and I shall write you the final letter, and I shall see you no more. I told you that much yesterday evening, and still I write it to you again. Yes, for the reason I treated you falsely last night, and I left you with a different impression, and I wouldput that right. You acted so differently from your nature that I forgive you, and even went so far as to bring my mind to bear how I could take you back again. First, the devil stood behind, and my better reason gave way for the moment and I came away, telling you I would see you no more. When your better character comes in contact with mine, we are so much alike that much of what is said, like that last night, had better been unsaid. All now looks bright and beautiful, and my better nature trembles at the ideas that were expressed last night. But that I should have left on your mind an idea that you could control me is erroneous. There are truths in this affair, and they must be spoken. You have gone out from one element and have taken another (Stokes), and for you to turn back, either when you are situated that way, or when even you could say that element had gone, should make no difference to me. It was you that took the step, and you should and shall suffer the consequences. Supposing the part you took last night and yesterday afternoon was one of truth, if not, and I——

Again, if you was not dealing from your heart in what took place, and I hope it was not true, then there are no consequences and no suffering for you to endure. Why, it has been many a long year since I could say to myself that I had committed such a folly. To find another like yesterday would bring me back almost to childhood. To imagine that I should have again crossed your threshold, and crossed it, too, deliberately, knowing that the same facts existed that had given me all my trouble and made me this sorrow—why, it is devilish. I told you that I had passed the realm where I had forgiven you all the sorrow you had made me, and that I would not murmur; I would not find fault with all that I saw. I would fain tear your image from my mind, and I will. Why, I thought all night last night and all day to-day of your saying, "I would rather be a toad," &c., &c. Was that written to apply to me? I should say so. Yes. Who knows what you would not conceive. No one but yourself. And I must weigh you carefully, for I have nothing but a great character to deal with, and I must meet things carefully. You might suppose you could love two, and, perhaps, more elements, and make them hover near you. Certainly you did last night, and, for shame, I was one of them. But it will *never* occur again. For once let us be honest. You went that road because it looks smooth and pleasant, and mine looked ragged and worn. Now, a mistake cannot be found out too soon. Travel further along, and don't try to turn so soon. I can see you now, as you were last night, when you talked of this man (Stokes); and do not deceive yourself—*you love him.* Yesterday there was nothing but the breaking up of strong pride and the giving way of wilfulness. Cling to that one. Leave me alone, for in me you have *nothing left.* Why ask me to weaken yourself with him? All this you must study; but I pledge you to-night that I will not countenance even your impression on my mind until the door is closed behind him forever. For what you can gain from me you probably cannot afford to do that; so let me advise you—nourish him and be careful. Nothing is so bad for you as changes. He loves you; you love him. You have caused me all the misery you could. Cling to him. Be careful what you do, for he will be watchful. How well he knows *you cheated me.* He will look for the same. And now, as I know precisely how you stand from your own lips, I will treat him differently. Although you would not protect him, I will. While he is there, and until his memory is buried forever, never approach me, for I shall send you away unseen. Ever be careful that you do not have the feeling that you can come back to me, for there is a wide gulf between you and me. I would not hold a false hope out to you. I shall not trouble you more in this letter. You have the only idea I can express to you. You know when you can see me again, if ever. The risk for you is too great. Loving and suited as you are, cling to him for the present, and when your nature gets tired of that throw him off. And so long until it is time for you to be weary and for you to be "put in your little bed" forever, you must rest contented. Don't begin plotting to-morrow. Take to-morrow for thought, and be governed by this letter, for the writer has much of your destiny in his hands.

JOSIE STILL CLINGS TO FISK.

Notwithstanding their last farewell letter, Josie still clung to Fisk. She asked him for favors, asked him for money, which Fisk, in

MRS. JOSIE MANSFIELD. 107

his good nature, almost always gave, as we see by the letter following:

November 1, 1870.

MISS MANSFIELD—I have taken the steps for the corn doctress' removal to a southern clime, where her business should be better, as vegetables of that class thrive more rapidly there than on our bleak shores. I presume it will take from two, or say four days, before I get the passes, when they will be sent to you. Should she call on you say to her to come back in four days and you will have them for her. I sent you a package by Maggie for what you desired on Saturday evening, with a little surplus over for trimmings, which I hope you received. I am of your opinion regarding not only Dr. Pape, but all of the doctors. You are well; let nature take its course. You are in too good health to tamper with a constitution as good as yours. This is important for your consideration. Yours, truly,

JAMES.

November 10, 1870.

Enclosed find $300. Please use. I am very sorry we could not have arrived at a more satisfactory conclusion last night. I did all I could, and the same feeling prevails o'er me now. With a careful and watchful manner you should look at all our affairs. You should make no mistake. You told me I should hear from you when you came to a conclusion. Therefore I wait upon your early reply, and until then I must, of course, pursue the same course I have for the last six weeks. I hope we shall mutually understand each other, for the thing could be made, as should be made, satisfactory to you. I am, yours, JAMES.

MORE MONEY TO JOSIE.

Fisk sent $1,000 to Josie in November, with this memorandum:
Erie Railway Company, Treasurer's Office, November 1, 1870, receiving desk—$500.

WM. H. B.

Erie Railway Company, Treasurer's Office, November 10, 1870, receiving desk—$500.

WM. H. B.

Please acknowledge receipt. JAMES.

November 11, 1870.

Enclosed you will find the order on Miss Guthrie, which have Etta or you present and it will be all right. Mr. Comer gave them an order not to deliver anything only on my written order to stop the "opera bouffers," but present this enclosed order and it will be all right. Mrs. Reher was here this morning and I gave her transportation for herself and Michael to Charlestown by steamer.

Enclosed you will find box at theatre in order to get the same, as it was sold. I have convinced myself that I desire you and yours to come.

Please answer the note, that I may know you are to come.

Yours, truly, JAMES.

November 12, 1870.

Enclosed find the letters. I was not aware Miss Jordan was to come until I saw her pass the gate-keeper, but that is nothing astonishing, as she is one of our regular customers. Of course I did not send her the box for she is not in a mood that I presume such civilities would be received from Fisk, Jr. I am glad you was pleased. I would have been glad to have you seen "Le Petit Faust." At the "Duchesse" we used old clothes and scenery, while in "Faust" all was new. We play "Faust" this afternoon. Shall I send you a box? And on Monday night we give the world "our diamond," "Les Brigands," all new.

Surely the world is machinery. Am I keeping up with it? is the question. Yours truly, JAMES.

FISK'S BOYISHNESS.

We now find Fisk completely melted again and still in love with the woman to whom he had written such severe letters, Josie never gave him up. She kept in his way. By and by Fisk's love came back by degrees, and we now see him writing as fondly as ever:

November 14, 1870.

DEAR DOLLY—Do you really wish to see a "brigand" at your house to-night? If so, what hour, or from what hour and how late should I call? for I might be able to come at eight, or perhaps not until ten. Say what hour, and how late is your limit after the time you first say.

NOVEMBER 15, 1870.

Enclosed find box for to-night. Should you find you cannot use it send it back in letter. Do you feel as I said you would this morning? The box, of course, is for whoever you may invite.

Yours, ever, JAMES.

NOVEMBER 16, 18—.

DEAR DOLLY—Don't feel that way. Go riding, and to-night, darling, I will take you to rest. I shall go out at half-past three, and you can safely look ahead, darling, for rest. It will come, and we shall be happy again.   Yours, truly,   JAMES.

NOVEMBER 18, 1870.

Shall go to the race to-day, and this evening I am engaged until late, and I am afraid you would get tired waiting for the ring of the bell or the ring of the door. So I will not ask you to wait my coming unless it be your wish, in which case I will come as early as I can.
Enclosed find the Leidunnor Ball.   Yours, truly,
J. F., JR.

MONDAY MORNING.
Not time to come up.   J. F., JR.

THE STOKES SUIT.

After Fisk and Josie had "made up," Stokes entered the field again. He persuaded Josie that the letters which Fisk had written were of immense value to him, and that he would pay any price rather than have them exposed to the gaze of the public. So in a fatal hour Josie consented to "go back" on Fisk.

Fisk received this copy of his private correspondence with the woman whom he had once loved, whom he had taken from poverty and made rich, with a feeling of remorse. He had no resentment. He saw their object and met their attack at once. He immediately, to make sure that he was right, sent for Richard E. King, a colored boy in the employ of Josephine Mansfield. Richard is an intelligent boy. He testified that he had overheard Stokes and Josephine Mansfield talk about the scheme of getting money out of Fisk. Stokes said he "was going for $100,000." Richard heard it and came and told Fisk. Fisk caused Richard to make an affidavit as to what he had heard Stokes say, which affidavit has been published. For this affidavit Stokes commenced a suit against Fisk for libel, which will be spoken of hereafter.

Stokes now failing to get a settlement from Fisk for his $200,000 claim, offered to enter upon an arbitration, and selected Clarence Seward to arbitrate the matter. Fisk agreed to this. Clarence Seward decided that Stokes' claim was null and void, but that Fisk ought to pay Stokes $10,000 damage for the night which he spent in the

Toombs. This Fisk agreed to do, provided Stokes would give up the letters which he had written to Josephine Mansfield. Stokes agreed to this and received the $10,000 from Wm. H. Morgan, Fisk's attorney, on the 30th of June, 1871. Stokes also wanted Fisk to pay his attorney, Ira Shafer, $5,000. This Fisk agreed to. So he paid in all to get these letters out of Stokes' hands $15,000, and Stokes sent the letters to Peter B. Sweeney, with this letter:

HON. PETER B. SWEENEY:

DEAR SIR—Mr. Buckley informed me of your desire to have possession of Mr. Fisk's letters, approved, &c. I herewith send them all to you. Yours respectfully,

NEW YORK, April 12, 1871. E. S. STOKES.

A release and award, which was to forever close the dispute, was given by Stokes to Fisk.

A New York correspondent, in speaking of this heroine in the dark, romantic reality which has achieved for her a notoriety which has by far eclipsed even her former unenviable fame, says that it was from Boston that she set out upon her conquering career; but in New York she found her most ample field, and gained her most substantial victories, in the half world of which she is the most illustrious figure. Occupying a brown-stone front house, on Twenty-third street, said to be the gift of the free-handed Fisk, she found means to gratify the most magnificent tastes. The fitting-up of this establishment is that of a palace. Laces and brocades fall in contrasting folds before the windows; mossy carpets cover the floor; the walls are hung with gems of choice paintings; the table furniture is the richest work of the silversmith. It is a petit *trianon*, according to the accounts of its favored visitors, and these, be it remembered, are not of plebeian station. The little supper at which the President himself, the guest of the hospitable Fisk, assisted under the smiles of the fair mistress of the mansion, has become part of history.

Her horses and carriages were the finest that pranced and rolled through the avenues to Central Park. At Long Branch, a four-in-hand, matched bays, alone sufficed for her ambition, and the liveried driver and footman were of the blackest hue, as well as the most skillful in their profession, to be obtained. Flashing over the solid roads of the Park, or trundling leisurely at the fashionable hour along the drives on the bluffs at the Branch, Miss Mansfield filled a place in the public eye allotted to objects of the greatest admiration. Even when called to court, the coupe in which she was rolled without a jolt over the pavement, trod by plebeian feet and showed luxurious cushions of crimson satin, clear glass windows, and a glittering body, whose gloss the coats of the gaily harnessed pair at the pole alone eclipsed. From this stepped the owner, clad in silk and velvet, fur seal cloak, and diamonds at ears, throat and wrists.

The woman who can command such resources must be a marvel. That she possesses a mysterious fascination, none who have ever witnessed her smiles or frowns will deny. A flourish of her delicate lace handkerchief has been known to soften the heart of a judge; a tear has melted a frigid cross-examiner; a toss of her jaunty jockey hat has been answered by a rustle of admiration throughout the court. But Miss Mansfield has in reality little beyond the freshness and vivacity of a youth not yet impaired to make up the sum of her true attractions. What is by courtesy styled *embonpoint* might without exaggeration be denominated grossness; what is intended as a languishing glance from her truly rich eyes, a detractor might call a leer; while her ripe and mobile mouth has already a hard set to its lines which is cruel to see. What Miss Mansfield will be when years have expanded her already broad figure, flattened her sensuous face, and wiped out the brightness which may now pass for intellect, is too apparent in the woman as she now appears. The diamonds that she wears in a profusion that indicate the fancy of the woman, are real, and will retain their glitter; but she herself is paste only, coarse-grained, and ready to dull into worthlessness.

And so we close this page of a life of which nothing good can be said. Beautiful, selfish, treacherous, we can only despise and abhor the creature whose duplicity and wanton wickedness destroyed the friendship which existed between Colonel Fisk and Edward Stokes, costing one his life, and leaving the other a wreck. God grant there be few like her.

THE LIFE, CAREER, AND CHARACTER OF

Edward S. Stokes,

THE ASSASSIN.

CHAPTER I.

HIS EARLY LIFE—PHILADELPHIA REMINISCENCES—SPORTING PROCLIVITIES—HIS RELATIONS WITH MANSFIELD—HIS CONNECTION WITH FISK—HIS LAWYERS—THE LINE OF DEFENSE—HIS FAMILY AND FRIENDS.

Edward S. Stokes was born in Philadelphia in the year 1841, and is consequently in his thirty-first year. His parents, who were possessed of a moderate fortune, and moved in the best society, removed to New York in 1850. He received an excellent classical and English education at the Philadelphia High School. He acquired knowledge readily, but was especially noted for his fondness for athletic sports, in which he always excelled. From early youth he is said to have exhibited a fierceness of passion and ungovernable temper, amounting at times almost to insanity. Always sensitive to insult, and quick to resent an injury, he has frequently involved himself in serious difficulties. He began life as a clerk in his father's provision establishment in Chambers street, and showed considerable business tact and ability. Stokes is five feet nine inches high, and weighs about one hundred and forty pounds. He is slightly built, but is very wiry and active on his feet. In conversation he talks quickly and to the point, and hurries his affairs through as rapidly as possible. Stokes is a man of

EDWARD S. STOKES, The Assasin.

STOKES, THE ASSASSIN.

FINE APPEARANCE,

of a dark complexion, with piercing black eyes, and regular features. His hair, which was jet black a couple of years ago, is now partly gray, and were it not for his active movements he would pass for a man of forty-five years. Mr. Stokes married a lady of good family some ten years ago, and has by her one child, a very beautiful girl of nine years of age. In June of last year, Mrs. Stokes, who was in bad health, visited Europe to seek some benefit from the mineral springs of Central Germany, and when last heard from, as late as December 3, was in Paris. The family, while in New York, had an elegant suite of apartments at the Worth House, corner of Fifth Avenue and Twenty-sixth street. These apartments were furnished with every article of luxury and refinement that taste could devise or that money could buy

Nearly two years ago Stokes became acquainted with Fisk, and engaged with him in various business enterprises. Through Mr. Fisk he formed the acquaintance of Helen Josephine Mansfield, the *ci-devant* wife of an actor. An intimacy sprung up between the two, which has just resulted in the tragic death of Mr. Fisk.

THE SUITS AND COUNTER-SUITS

between Fisk on the one hand, and Mansfield and Stokes on the other hand, have occupied the courts, and filled the columns of the newspapers for a year past. Stokes accused Fisk of endeavoring to deprive him of property to the amount of $200,000, which he had accumulated in the oil refining business. This charge was repelled by Fisk, who arrested Stokes on a charge of fraud. The fraud not being proven, the latter was released, and brought suit against Fish for false imprisonment. The litigations growing out of this and other causes have continued without interruption for nearly twelve months past.

These expensive proceedings have rapidly absorbed the remainder of Stokes's fortune, and it is said that he would not have been able to maintain the fight longer from lack of funds. He has expended nearly forty thousand dollars in lawyers' fees alone, in the hope that he would recover ten times that amount from Fisk. The quarrel has undoubtedly been stimulated and the fued increased by Mrs. Mansfield, who was herself pecuniarily interested in the result of the proceedings.

STOKES'S COUNSEL—WHO THEY ARE.

Sunday morning, as soon as Stokes heard of the death of his victim, he sent for Hon. John McKeon, his counsel. Afterwards he sent for Mr. W. O. Bartlett and his son, and John Graham.

MR. M'KEON

is one of the oldest and shrewdest members of the New York bar, a man of great tact, much culture and extended experience. He is pugnacieus to a degree, and has had many a battle with the fraternity. one of the most virulent being when, with his brother Graham, he fought the Strong divorce case against Mr. Cram, before Judge Garvin, in the superior court. He has been the counsel of Stokes in all the Fisk suits.

MR. BARTLETT

is one of the clearest-headed men living. He is an expert rather than a lawyer, and is versed in all the technicalities of practice, full of resorts, and up in everything likely to make or mar a cause. His son is rapidly earning a reputation with his father.

JOHN GRAHAM

is the Boanerges of the bar, a tremendous trip-hammer of a fellow, who never hesitates to take a chance, and never fears an opponent. He is probably the best criminal advocate in the country, and has a wreath of laurels big enough for the most ambitious

FURTHER PARTICULARS.

The Styles family of Philadelphia, to which Mr. Stokes, through his mother' side, belongs, is one of the oldest and most intensely respectable families in the Quaker City. By blood and by marriage, Mr. Stokes is also connected with several of the most influential families and firms in New York city. Notably, Phelps, Dodge & Co., Henry Stokes, of the Manhattan company; Clinton Gilbert, of the Greenwich Savings Institution, and others.

His father-in-law, John W. Southwick, is a millionaire, a retired furniture dealer, residing on Fifth avenue, and will spare no expense to secure the acquittal of the murderer.

While in Philadelphia, Stokes attended and graduated at the High school, under Professor Hart, and developed quite a taste for *Belles-Lettres*. Strange to say, he cares not a rush for poetry.

He admires Addison, Steele, Goldsmith and Irving, but utterly fails to appreciate Shelly or Byron.

His favorite Philadelphia resort was Barret's gymnasium, where he took boxing lessons, and acquired great proficiency in the manly art of self-defense. It is a pity for all parties that he took the pistol to redress his wrongs—he should have used the fist.

Fisk would have been almost equally in his power, and society and his soul would have been spared a crime.

Mr. Stokes was also addicted to horse-flesh, and quite a rivalry has existed between Mr. Smith, of the firm of Smith Gould & Martin, and himself, in regard to the respective speed of their nags. This rivalry has culminated in a dispute regarding "time," which is still unsettled.

Tom Warner, the well-known Erie broker has also been engaged in horse contests with Stokes, the results of which still remain in a state unsatisfactory for all parties.

Mr. Stokes is well known abroad—having been several times in Europe, where he has resided in London, Paris, Vienna, and the other large capitals. In Paris he was very popular with the American colony, and in London was received with more favor than is accorded to the average Americans.

His adventures in Vienna were many and romantic, and he is the hero of several continental episodes.

It is claimed, by the friends of Stokes, that he was a rich man prior to his introduction to Fisk, and that it was the latter who solicited his acquaintance.

It is also stated that Mr. Fisk, from the first, used Stokes as his tool, and determined to "bleed" him, and that ere long Mr. Stokes found that Fisk had conceived the idea of appropriating his (Stokes) oil works to his own benefit.

THE LINE OF DEFENSE.

The ground upon which Mr. Stokes' lawyers stand in their attempts to save their client's life, now in jeopardy, from the law embraces the following four points :

1. They will attempt to show that Mr. Fisk had, by his persecutions, driven Stokes into a species of monomania, under the influence of which he committed the fatal deed.

2. They will try to show that Stokes did *not* lie in wait for Mr. Fisk, but was at the Grand City Hotel on some private business, during which he chanced, unexpectedly, to encounter his enemy.

3. They will still further attempt to prove that Mr. Fisk himself

was armed, and cherished ideas of inflicting personal violence upon Stokes; and that he had people in his employ who were to dispose of Stokes just as Mr. Norman B. Eaton had been disposed of by the Erie gang previously.

4. They will finally try to show that the wounds inflicted upon the person of Mr Fisk by Mr. Stokes, were not necessarily mortal, but that if they had been properly treated, which they were not, Mr. Fisk would have recovered.

What success these lawyers will meet with in following out their line of defense remains to be seen.

THE HOME OF EDWARD S. STOKES.

The writer called at the residence of Mr. Edward S. Stokes, No. 23 West Forty-ninth Street, one evening. In answer to the summons of the bell the door was opened by a younger brother of the prisoner, and he was invited to come in.

On entering the elegant parlor, it was apparent that a pall hung over the little household. The father, a pleasant, elderly gentleman, came forward and extended his hand to the writer, and said, "I presume, sir, you have called relative to the unfortunate affair of Saturday, in which my son Edward was concerned, and who languishes in prison for his rashness under a momentary insanity in which he took the life of Col. Fisk. Ah! my dear sir," he said, "this is terrible."

"Yes, I can imagine your anguish," answered the writer. "Have you no theory as to the motive which prompted your son to commit the terrible act?"

"No; as I am totally ignorant of the affair; I have not seen my son since."

"Do *you* think Mrs. Mansfield is much to blame?"

"I do not know the woman, and have never seen her. I have only read of her in the newspapers. Our family are just as ignorant as the public in the details of the death of Col. Fisk."

"Your son, I presume, always bore a good character previous to his connection with Fisk and Mrs. Mansfield?"

"Always, sir; he was a dutiful and obedient boy, and never was the cause of any sorrow to his family until this fatal infatuation. I have endeavored, whenever he has referred to these suits against Fisk, to dissuade him from his purpose to follow them up, and to let the matter of Fisk's persecution of him alone. Whenever I spoke he would fly into a frenzied passion."

"Have you detected anything wrong about him, or that he was depressed in spirits?"

"Yes, frequently of late I have observed him to act very strangely, and he appeared to be

DERANGED IN HIS MIND.

These suits have preyed upon him to such an extent that he was not the same person, and would listen to no advice."

"But the public are very much incensed at the wanton, cruel and unprovoked murder which he has committed in slaying a fellow-being and sending his soul into eternity without a moment's warning."

"I am conscious of the enormity of the crime," answered the stricken father, "but Edward was never known to harbor the least antipathy toward any person, nor was he ever heard to express any malice toward those whom he considered his enemies. The community, I know, are very indignant at the awful tragedy, but I pray that they will not prejudge my son, but that they will

SUSPEND THEIR MALEDICTIONS

on his head until he has made a statement in extenuation of his crime. There are developments which will be adduced, and which will considerably alter the feeling against him."

Mrs. Stokes, the mother, was walking the floor with her two sons who were speaking words of consolation to her and trying to soothe her affliction. The family were all composed, and betrayed no emotion except their actions, which plainly told that they were trying to conceal their grief.

A few days since, the writer of these lines visited his former acquaintance, Edward S. Stokes, in his cell in the Toombs. He experienced some difficulty in "getting at" the prisoner, as he was surrounded, absolutely besieged by his friends, as well as constantly in communication with his counsel. Among the visitors were the proprietors of several Broadway hotels, two or three *sports*, several young men about town, three or four merchants, and a prominent lawyer.

Mr. Stokes evidently enjoyed the liberty of the prison, and was allowed every privilege that was not incompatible with duty and precaution.

After waiting half an hour or so, we were admitted to the presence, and found Mr. Stokes on the second corridor of the prison, occupying cell No. 56, until his own cell, No. 50, was properly fitted up for his accommodation. He was elegantly attired in his usual morning costume, a smoking-cap, a velvet jacket, light loose pantaloons, silk stockings and embroidered slippers, and was busily employed smoking a first-class cigar, and chatting with his friends.

But with all this, there was not the slightest degree of pretence or of affectation. He was dressed just as he always dressed at home, and was doing just what he always did at home in the morning—nothing. Right or wrong, in good taste or bad, he was in his prison what he had always been in his hotel—a gentleman—neither more or less, and there was nothing more to be said about it.

As for the cell which he had fitted up so gorgeously, *a la* newspaper reports, let us describe it as we saw it.

A few yards of cheap carpet, a few yards of cheap paper, a cheap stove, a small iron bed, with a hair mattrass and a "fancy" coverlid, and clean sheets, a wash-stand of the simplest description, a small, plain table, a small mirror, a three-shelved rack, containing on the lower shelf a dozen bottles of cologne and Florida water, a bouquet, a shaving tumbler and apparatus; on the middle shelf some combs and brushes, a cigar-box, and a lamp; and on the top shelf, a number of novels, while on the cupboard lay a tray with some dishes, glasses, some fruit, and some game. These, with a cane and a portrait of himself, hanging from some pegs on the wall, in company with the identical light pants and overcoat which he wore at the time of the murder, completed the contents of this "gorgeous" cell—all the "palatial" splendor of which could have been purchased for two hundred dollars.

This may be "luxury," but if it is, then luxury is cheap. For our part, for the life of us, we could not see any "bad taste," any "defying of public sentiment," any "violation of prison rules," about it; it seemed the most natural thing in the world that a man of a certain social class having been taken to prison, should take the habit and the surroundings, and the customs and costumes of his class there with him, while as far as the prison officials are concerned, until a man was really a convict, that is to say, had really been tried and *convicted* of a crime, he had a perfeet right to dress or live as he pleased—provided he could afford to pay for it.

Mr. Stokes was very cool, calm, and collected. He betrayed no nervousness, and talked freely. He spoke of Mr. Fisk as a bad man, a false friend, and a base intriguer, but disclaimed ever entertaining any personal malice against him, and vowed that he never knowingly would have harmed a hair of his head. He regarded " Mrs. Mansfield as a good-hearted and well-meaning woman ;" " as a woman who would have loved Fisk, if Fisk would have let her;" while of his own little daughter he spoke in terms of the most affectionate endearment,

Listening to his soft, low voice; looking into his soft, dark eyes; watching his mobile, handsome face, one could scarcely fancy that he was the murderer of James Fisk, Jr.

After a while, the crowd of visitors to the prison thinned, the convicts were fed, just as the beasts are in their cages, the prisoners were exercised, and walked through the corridors, the declining sun shown in more faintly "between the bars," and still Stokes sat in his cell with his friends and smoked, and chatted, until his father came— a venerable-looking old gentleman—with a friend of the prisoner's, and then we and our companions resigned our places to the newcomers, and bade "Ned" Stokes good-bye.

Stokes has been arranged on an indictment found by the Grand Jury, but he has not yet pleaded. Everything was in a muddle in New York, there was two Grand Juries. It is the common opinion of the Bar that one of these bodies was illegal. As Mr. Stokes counsel have not decided whether to plead to the indictment or demur, it was quite probable that a new indictment would be found after one of the Grand Juries should have been discharged. There are some interesting if not startling positions taken for the defence. The one is that Colonel Fisk was not only armed, but that the wound in his body was inflicted by himself—inflicted *a la* Vallandigham, in attempting to draw his pistol from his pocket. That two pistols were used is very clear, from the fact that two bullets were found, one in Fisk's body and one on the marble pavement, the one bullet fitting the pistol found and the other not. The bullet on the body fitting the pistol found, the bullet on the floor, which produced the wound in the arm, not fitting any pistol yet produced. The theory is that Fisk, coming in at the door and seeing Stokes on the stairs, attempted to draw his pistol, when it accidentally discharged at the same moment when he received Stokes' bullet in the arm.

The parties who removed the outside clothing of the Colonel are yet to be produced in Court. The woman who handed the pistol to the officer is yet to tell how it came into her hands, with other interesting testimony to show that Stokes did not fire on an unarmed man. But two witnessed the shooting. These were two hall-boys of the Central Hotel, who were either so frightened that they did not know what was going on, or deliberately perjured themselves, as they flatly contradicted each other and their own testimony on the stand. In the proper time and before the proper tribunal, the action of the Coroner's jury will be tested. Above all, the proceedings of the jury in consultation will be investigated. One man on the jury was not summoned. He came unsolicited. He said he was on the Matthews inquest, understood such matters, and wanted to go on the jury; so he sat at the inquest. He was found to be a special enemy of Stokes, and pledged to look after the interests of Colonel Fisk. On entering the room for consultation, the jury were presented with a verdict, drawn up in the strong form of an indictment, in which the shooting was set forth as "killing with malice aforethought," and other well-known phrases of an indictment. On this verdict the jury were divided, six and six. The gentleman referred to, acting as counsel, insisted upon the adoption of the verdict with its strong phrases as the only thing that would satisfy an indignant public. Others contended that the object of the inquest was not to try Stokes—not to anticipate his defence, but simply to ascertain how Fisk came to his death. The debate lasted over three hours, and ended in a compromise by which the word "deliberate" was added to the simple phraseology of the verdict.

CHAPTER II.

THE FISK MURDER—STOKES' AFFIDAVIT.

At the arraignment of Stokes before the Court of Oyer and Terminer, New York, January 29, the following affidavit was presented by Stokes' counsel:

City and County of New York, ss.: Edward S. Stokes, the defendant above named, being duly sworn, deposes and says: That, as he is informed by two of his counsel (Messrs. Wm. O. Bartlett and John Graham) and verily believes, they called upon Coroner Young at his residence, No. 107 King street, in the city of New York, on the afternoon of the 7th inst., a few hours after the death of James Fisk, Jr., to ascertain when the inquest would be held upon his body; that they were politely received by the said coroner, to whom they apologized for intruding themselves upon him on a Sabbath afternoon, and that he immediately became very communicative to them as to the manner in which he intended to conduct the inquest. That he stated he had gone over the City Directory and himself selected the names of respected citizens or members of the community, from whom he proposed forming his jury, and that they had been picked out with reference to their supposed inacquaintance with either party, and their supposed fairness and disinterestedness; that he had himself no feeling in the matter either way; that he meant to perform his duty impartially, and that he meant to get out the whole truth, no matter whom it affected; that this last expression he repeated and emphasized several times, sometimes using the words, "all the truth," sometimes the words, "all the facts," seeming to want to impress upon this deponent's said two counsel the conviction that this deponent should have the most complete justice done to him by that investigation; giving him to understand that he intended to devote all the time to the investigation requisite to bring forward all the testimony which could by any possibility throw light upon the occurrence. That he stated when he first became coroner, the coroner's office enjoyed a bad reputation, and that he had resolved from the start to perform his official duty solely under the guidance of his official oath; that he had been in several instances offered or given to understand that he could have money, but that the attempts to pass upon him were unavailing; that he was commencing to dilate upon his views or understanding about the law governing coroner's juries, when he was checked by one of the said two counsel, who remarked to him that it would not be proper to extend the conversation further, and that whatever further was said or done by him, or to or with him, had better be in the regular course of legal proceedings, when all parties would be within the view and hearing of the public.

And the deponent further saith, that before the testimony was gone into at all before the Coroner's jury on the afternoon of the 8th inst., (which was the first day of the proceedings,) one of the deponent's counsel addressed the Coroner, intending to urge upon him two matters preliminary, one of which, on account of the interruption and apparent unwillingness of the Coroner to listen to him, as the same counsel has informed this deponent, and, as he believes, he was unable to suggest to the Coroner at all; that the two matters were:

First. The propriety of exhausting all the evidence attainable as to the condition of the deceased at the very time he was shot, was to place beyond all doubt the fact as to whether the deceased was himself armed at that point of time or not.

Second. That the statutes did not require the Coroner to make return of his proceedings to the Court before the first Monday of February next, which gave him an ample opportunity to proceed with the inquest in the most deliberate manner, enabling him to elicit the whole truth, as he had promised he would in the conversation of the previous afternoon, above referred to. That the second of these matters was not alluded to at that stage of the proceedings, and for the reason already stated, as this deponent is informed by the counsel who addressed the Coroner, and as he verily believes. And this deponent further saith that the annexed schedule, marked "A," contains a report of the proceedings before the Coroner's jury, on the afternoon of the 8th and 9th instant, as cut from one of the daily newspapers published in the city of New York, and that, so far as it goes, it appears to be substantially correct.

And this deponent further saith that the annexed schedule, marked "B," contains the *ante-mortem* statement of James Fisk, Jr., claimed to have been taken on the afternoon of the 6th instant, with the verdict of the coroner's jury thereupon, as copied from one of the daily newspapers published in the city of New York.

And this deponent further saith that the annexed schedule, marked "C," contains a list of the names of the jurors selected for the inquest upon the dead body of the deceased, as copied from one of the daily newspapers published in the city of New York, and announced as the names from which the final jury would be drawn.

And this deponent further saith that, from the manner in which the coroner spoke at the close of the proceedings before the last mentioned jury, his counsel indulged the hope that he would defer making a return of his proceedings to the court of trials until the latest moment, *i. e.*, the first Monday of February next, the consideration having been strongly pressed upon him that, during the first stages of the public excitement, any undue haste would, or might, be regarded as deferring to such a feeling, when sound legal policy dictated the contrary course.

And this deponent further saith that upon the final jury, as constituted, Maunsell B. Field was placed, whose name does not appear in the list of jurors set out in schedule "C," and that this deponent has been informed, and verily believes he came forward at the last moment almost voluntarily, and was put upon the jury at his own request.

And this deponent further saith, that another of the jurors, Mr. James R. Edwards, was a friend of the deceased, and had transacted business for him in his lifetime, as this deponent has been informed and believes; and that both he and Mr. Field (who is a lawyer) were active in the jury-room in trying to procure the most unfavorable verdict to their deponent they could, from their previous sympathies with the deceased, as this deponent has been informed and verily believes.

That as this deponent has been informed and verily believes a proposed verdict was secretly handed to one of the jurors, or sent into the jury room, or prepared in advance by one of them, and carried in by him, which, if adopted by them, would have incorporated into their finding the words "felonious," "premeditated," and "malice aforethought," or similar words of the most prejudicial character to deponent, and that this was done with the knowledge and approval of the Coroner, notwithstanding the remonstrance of this deponent's counsel protesting that the facts placed before the jury were garbled, and not such as were within the power and control of the Coroner, if he really intended that the jury should have the whole truth.

And this deponent further saith that the indictment pending against him in this Court was, as he distinctly believes and charges, hurried through, through the instrumentality of private counsel connected with the prosecution nominally in behalf of the relatives of the deceased, but in reality representing other parties largely interested in business with the deceased in his lifetime, and who, with the deceased, were inimical to the deponent, not from any wrong he did them, but because he was familiar with transactions in which they had been jointly concerned, the exposure of which they justly dreaded.

And this deponent further saith that, as he has been informed, and verily believes, James Fisk, Jr., the deceased, as a matter of mere malice and revenge, ignoring the Police Court altogether, went before the Grand Jury of this Court, empanelled at its last December term, and falsely and wickedly made a complaint against this deponent and one Helen Josephine Mansfield for a conspiracy. That the said Grand Jury was, as this deponent has been informed and verily believes, largely composed of the personal friends of the deceased, or those who were in the control of those friends, and that they are the same Grand Jury who found the indictment in question against this deponent. That, in the judgment of this deponent's counsel, even supposing them to be perfectly disinterested and impartial otherwise, after having been poisoned or prejudiced against this deponent by the false and calumnious statements of the deceased and his witnesses to sustain the manufactured charge of conspiracy against him and the said Mansfield, they were not a proper body to pass upon the subject of the indictment in question.

And this deponent further saith that, as he had been informed, and verily believes, the manufactured complaint of conspiracy was continued before the Grand Jury, after the death of the said Fisk, and, as he charges and believes, with a view to prejudicing him under the present indictment for homicide, and depriving him of the testimony of the said Mansfield, if she should be used as a witness in his behalf under the present indictment by disparaging or blackening her, so that he would not dare to resort to her as a witness.

That among other witnesses before the grand jury in reference to this charge of conspiracy, as this deponent has been informed and verily believes, appears the name of William Fullerton, Esq., who, in the *post mortem* proceedings before the coroner's jury, appeared as, or was assumed to be, one of the private counsel against this deponent; that this deponent had previously employed Mr. Fullerton as a counsel in the lifetime of the deceased in litigations which arose between them, and had paid him a counsel fee of $500, and that subsequently a demand was made upon this deponent by Mr. Fullerton for $5,000 additional for professional services, which claim this deponent refused to comply with or recognize, since which time Mr. Fullerton has been unfriendly to him; that on or about the 4th day of January, 1872, a summons and complaint was served upon this deponent in favor of Mr. Fullerton, of which a copy is herewith annexed, marked schedule "D;" that the award spoken of in the complaint was only $10,000 altogether; that Mr. Fullerton is possessed of many valuable secrets of this deponent, through his relation of counsel to this deponent, growing out of or affecting the relations and transactions of the deceased and this deponent, and that, notwithstanding this and the hostile attitude he has placed himself in, in suing this deponent for an unjust claim, he has been, as this deponent has been informed and verily believes, actively engaged in supervising the proceedings leading to the indictment in question, and preparing the case for the prosecution thereunder; that this deponent can attach no other explanation to his appearing in the grand jury room as a pretended witness in the charged of conspiracy above referred to, than the opportunity it gave him of exerting his influence and power as a counsel against him.

And this deponent further saith, that, as he has been informed and verily believes, an indictment was preferred against him and the said Mansfield, in this court, upon the said manufactured charge of conspiracy, on or about the 10th inst.

And this deponent further saith that, as he has been informed and verily believes, and as he understands will appear by the minutes of the Grand Jury, no further witnesses or testimony were or was furnished to or taken before that body than to or before the Coroner's Jury.

And this deponent further saith that, as he has been informed and verily believes, a Grand Jury for the Count of New York was duly empanelled in the Court of General Sessions of the Peace, in and for the City and County of New York, on Nov. 7, 1871; that its sessions were, on Nov. 29, 1871, continued, by an order of the Court to Dec., 1871, from which day they were similarly extended to Dec. 30, 1871, from which day they were similarly extended to Jan. 27, 1872. Thus, as this deponent has been informed and verily believes, this Grand Jury were actually in session on Jan. 12, 1872, the day the indictment in question was ordered against this deponent by the body claiming to be the Grand Jury of this Court.

That W. H. Morgan, whose name appears as a witness on the minutes of the Grand Jury, in reference to the false charge of conspiracy, did heretofore, as deponent is advised and believes, appear as counsel for said James Fisk on a motion before Justice Brady of the Supreme Court, on the first day of December last past, and made an affidavit against this deponent.

That subsequently the summons referred to in schedule " D " bearing the name of said Morgan, as attorney for said Fullerton, was served on deponent. E. S. STOKES.

JAY GOULD.

The names of Gould and Fisk have been so long inseparable that it seems scarcely possible to close this work, and think its pages complete, without some few comments, hasty and imperfect though they may, and must be, upon his business life and character. Almost from the first day of Fisk's public career, we find them associated together, and with the one exception that virtue is the opposite of vice, they were opposed to each other in everything. Perhaps it may be that in their very opposite qualities of mind and person, was to be found the charm which drew and bound them so closely together. Fisk is said to have been a very handsome man; if so, his was the Saxon type of beauty: while Gould, though fine looking, is decidedly Jewish in feature and expression, with dark, sallow, olive skin, piercing, yet restless eyes that never say "Look through me into heart and soul," jetty hair and beard, and is straight, lithe, sinewy, and restless. He is cool and cautious in business, not given to rash speculations, but deliberating, and weighing carefully his chances before embarking in enterprise. He plodded slowly and surely up the steep to success, while Fisk, taking in the situation at one quick glance, above, below, and around, caught the first projecting circumstance that offered a foothold, and with a leap and a bound, swung himself into the desired position. We often find ourselves admiring in another what we have no desire to imitate, so of Fisk's reckless movements, we admired in him, in an unbounded measure, the bold and daring maneuvers he knew he had not the ability to execute himself; and though he stood by in fear and trembling, and drew his breath fast through his tight set teeth, and was half paralyzed with terror, yet so sure was he that in some unforeseen way the tangled threads of the warp in the web he wove would be all straightened in the end, that beyond a half uttered remonstrance, he rarely interfered with his plans. His name, as a long established and well known financier, was a great help to the young specluator, and for a while lent an air of almost respectability to the too transparent frauds which were perpetrated by the younger member of the firm. In desparate straits there is little doubt but his courage was equal to Fisk's, though of a very different character. One could coolly "bide his time," counting his own and his adversary's strength, the other rushed headlong into the fray, trusting to the terror that his name inspired—to the good luck which usually attended him, or to something " turning up," by which he should be enabled to come off more than conqueror. As a broker in Erie stocks, he was often completely nonplused, and more than once, had he been left to manage the craft alone, there can be but little doubt she would have stranded. In their gold speculations his peculiar talents were brought into play, and it is more than likely he was the better man of the two, holding by his cool and concentrated powers what Fisk would have sacrificed in his impetuosity. It is well known that at last he wearied of his young, rash colleague, and that the bad odor which attached to Fisk's name sometimes led him to seriously consider the propriety of disengaging himself and his business from Fisk's, yet he was strongly attached to him, mourning his waywardness, and wondering at the fatal infatuation which bound him to a woman who was every day proving herself more and more unworthy of even such a love as he gave her. While, as I have said, he was in a way, attached to Fisk, I suppose it is in no way necessary to say that he used him constantly as a tool, and though he was the senior member of the firm, Fisk's name was kept before the public as the *active* agency, while he prudently remained in the background, in order that when public opinion was roused, and society must needs defend itself, and the hend of justice should fall, as fall it must, on the offender; why, *he* should stand safe sheltered from the punishment. Fisk has gone to a higher than man's tribunal. The impending blow was averted, and He who seeth not as man seeth, has taken the erring man to a different bar of justice. But with the gloom of the pall and the cerements of the grave around him, standing face to face with death in that most terrible form, under the shadow of the cypress and crape and nodding funeral plumes, he stood beside the body of his dead friend, looked long and silently into the face of the man who would never serve him more, and it is on record that "he turned away and wept bitterly."

SKETCH OF THE LIFE OF

WM. M. TWEED.

For the past year, indeed, for the past two years, no name has been so often and so unfavorably before the public as has the name of Wm. M. Tweed. Associated with every thing that was vile and low—a man in whom dwelt no principle of honor or honesty—a corrupt politician, he was yet the willing dupe and tool of men who were more base than himself, but, an apt scholar he proved himself to be, and soon became able to turn the tables in the most approved style, and was fully competent to show the late tutor a "trick worth two of his." Sprung into existence from the dregs of the very refuse of society, he is sufficiently base, ignorant, and degraded, to be a credit to the sinkhole of evil in which he was bred. All his instincts are brutal. All his aims are dishonorable. In his youth he worked at the trade of chairmaking, but this was a little too high up in the scale of honest industry, and no doubt he felt sadly out of his sphere, for he left it, and threw himself heart and soul into the more congenial profession of loafing, and was soon known as a confirmed vagrant, having neither home nor occupation. His first speculation was in chairs, and was typical of all later transactions. After starting a pretentious bogus business, and obtaining as large credit as his name could command, he "failed," leaving his creditors to mourn over their misplaced confidence, and firm believers in the too popular doctrine of total depravity. By the rule that "like attracts like," he became an object of interest to Boole and the gang of men who were engaged in a small way in the work of robbing the city. Tweed was relig-

HON. WM. M. TWEED.

iously strict in paying his devotions at the polls with the roughest of the professional roughs, and made himself so necessary to the corporation officers that to permanently secure his services, they finally gave him a foothold as one of their band. Ten years ago he was as bankrupt in purse as in moral character—without money, credit, or reputation—to-day he is worth millions of dollars, and boasts, regardless of the inference that must be drawn from it, that he owns more real estate, next to A. T. Stewart, than any other man in New York city.

The question naturally suggests itself to every mind, "How did he obtain his wealth." However he may be able to cheat justice of its dues, there is not one question left standing, or a doubt of which he can have the benefit, but that he is the most selfish, unscrupulous, rapacious thief of the quartette who rule the stricken and plundered city with a rod of iron. His first stroke of policy towards acquiring wealth and power was to secure his election to the State Senate. Familiar as he was with all the lowest and most desparate ruffians in the city, particularly in the district where he desired to run, and being too low and degraded to look to any other source for assistance, he had but to resort to such means as he had at his command. He also held at the same time the office of President of the old Board of Supervisors, which has been denounced as the most scandalously corrupt body that ever disgraced a community. By employing the same agencies that had hoisted him into power, he gradually worked his friends into positions where he could use them, and then commenced a scheme for surrounding every department in the government, of the city and country with a perfect network into whose meshes he could draw the revenues, and despoil the treasury at his leisure. The new Court House was a mine of wealth which Tweed and his accomplices worked as it pleased them. The very marble has netted them millions of dollars. From the old engine house, which they rented for a song, they received $5,000 per annum. He pays a most worthless paper over $1,000,000 per year for the city printing. This, of course, comes from the State Treasury, and is the sum given to hide from the world his frauds, false entries, and corrupt charges until such time as it is safe to defy the laws of the land. During the past two years he has drawn over $2,000,000 from the Treasury, for which he has returned no equivolent. Lies, fraud, forgery, are his never-varying, and never-failing resources, and there is no species of villiany that he is not familiar with, and capable

of embarking in, and this too without even the poor excuse of necessity
But the time came when the outraged people could endure no more
and for their own credit sake, were forced to take the matter into
their own hands, and seemed disposed to deal out retributive justice
in a manner suited to his crimes. Arrested as a felon—tried as a
felon—convicted as a felon, let us hope he will be forced to pay the
penalty of every misdeed. Ingersol, of whom every one has heard,
who has rendered his name infamous from its connection with
Tweed's, is a son of Lorin Ingersol, who in former years employed
Tweed in his chair manufactory. When Tweed run for senator.
Ingersol, Senior, assisted him to some money, in return for which he
put some "jobs" through the board of supervisors for Ingersol, and
took the son under his protection. The young Ingersol is said to
have evinced so great an aptitude for rascality as to be taken into
partnership with Tweed, and to have made vast sums of money, and
to be scarce inferior to Tweed. A nice pair of rogues are they, and
a credit to the school in which they graduated. Let us hope for the
sake of decency that the investigation will end in unearthing the
whole nest of rascals, thieves and criminals, and that there may be a
complete reform.

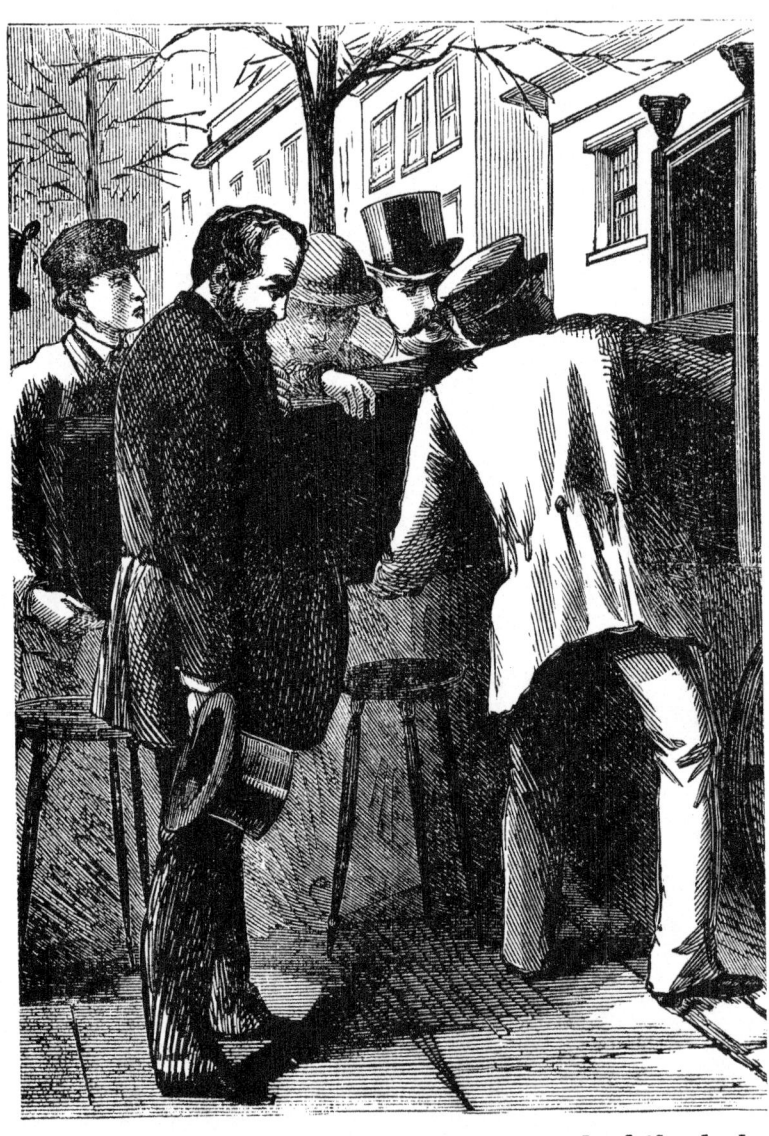

WM. M. TWEED attending the removal of the body of FISK from the Grand Central Hotel.

ANDREW J. GARVEY,

AND OTHER MEMBERS OF THE RING.

Keyser, Ingersol, McGregor, Mullally & Fields.

This is another of Tweed's accomplices. Like his patron and prototype, his early days were given to loafing and running to fires—he, too, being a "bunker" of the old fire department. At times he is said to have an industrious fit, when he would carry a hod, or do other labor for his brother, who was a plasterer. For this scoundrel of the deepest dye, Tweed discovered that he had a fellow feeling, which, we are told, makes us "wondrous kind," and he took the young bearer of the hod into his bosom and into his confidence, and from that time to the present they have worked with untiring industry for one common object, viz.: the depletion of the public purse. John H. Keyser is another of Tweed's *proteges*, and may be considered a real live Oily Gammon, an Amercanized specimen of the article—revised and improved in order to fit him to be a bright and shining light in the fraternity of which he is a member. Like Ingersol and Keyser, George Miller is another of the brood of young reptiles whom Tweed has nursed in his bosom, until they were able to go out and prey on the world. Mr Philip Lewis, a gentleman of the Israelitish persuasion, represents Mr. Tweed in the board of education. In addition to other sources of profit, Tweed started a breech-loading arms company, with James H. Ingersol for president, purchased a large lot of condemned muskets of the Allen pattern, and then smuggled through the legislature a bill making it obligatory on the authorities of the state to arm the National Guards with these worthless arms. He also bought out a bank, known as the Tenth National Bank, the operations of which have involved thousands of people in ruin. The terrible Black Friday of September, 1869, when the gold panic reached its climax and threatened to overwhelm the country, must be fresh in every mind. The well known "Ring" at that time consisted of Fisk, Gould, Tweed, Sweeny, and a host of the most corrupt and worthless men in America or any other country on the face of the round earth.

Tweed's "bosom friends" were legion, amongst whom were Billy Hickman, President of the board of Fire Commissioners, and Alex. Frear, holding the dual position of Commissioner of Charities and Correction (?), and Commissioner of Emigration. Frear is one of the most unprincipled scoundrels to be found in all the gang of disreputable knaves who have brought disgrace upon our public men. He has never been engaged in any ligitimate business, and can not hold a dollar of property in his own name, but he has amassed a large fortune by the most nefarious practice and is interested in every fraud that has been inangurated by the ring. Another pet of Tweed's, Mr. James McGregor, a Tammany Republican, is the head of the Department of Inspection of Buildings; while still another, Mr. Mullally, Editor of the Metropolitan Record, has been willing to abdicate his title as an honorable man and a good citizen, and become a member of the Board of Health, and a most suple tool and apologist for Tweed's confederates. Thomas C. Field is another of Tweed's "dear five hundred," and is one of the most efficient and unscrupulous tools of the Ring. He is a member of the Legislature, and is also Corporation attorney and a Commissioner of Public Parks. Three years ago Fields was so poor he could not pay his debts. To-day he is a wealthy man, having just completed a mansion valued at $600,000. It would be impossible in so small a space, to recount a hundredth part of the frauds and speculations in which this infamous Ring has been engaged, each only being more dark and nefarious than the other.

RICHARD B. CONNOLLY.

Richard B. Connolly was born in the county of Cork, Ireland, and might, on that acoount, be considered by vulgar minded people to belong to that large and respectable class of whom it has been said, with more force than elegance, "no rich need apply." An elder brother ("I said an *elder* soldier, *not* a *better* one") came to this country a good many years ago, and having succeeded, by the practice of a beautiful frugality which has never, to my knowledge, been practiced to any great extent by the younger scion of the family, in laying up a little money, he at once conceived the idea that a change of climate would be a good thing for the gentle Richard, and accordingly a message was sent across the broad blue ocean, bearing to him the invitation to bid adieu to the boys and weather of his native land, and come to the land of corn and wine, where there was bread (whiskey) and to spare. Of course the offer was accepted, but, alas, "man's base ingratitude to man makes countless thousands mourn," and amongst the mourners is the elder Connolly, for to this day the debt has never been canceled.

Richard early evinced a taste for politics, and before he had been in the country long enough to be entitled to vote, he succeeded in securing the nomination for county clerk, and was duly elected. The facility with which he made and broke promises, was his most marked characteristic, and so notorious did this practice become amongst his political associates, that he was unanimously accorded the marked distinction of being the most unmitigated liar in the community, and the pantonymic by which he had previously been known, soon gave place to the appropriate and significant cognomen of slippery Dick. The man who first applied the term to Connolly was a consummate judge of human nature, and hit the most appropriate term that could be applied to him, for in every position where he has been placed, he has proven himself to be indeed a "slippery" and unreliable man, and so convinced of this did his cronies become that they allowed a long series of years to elapse before he was again put forward for any political position.

At last, the Democratic party, forgetting that "in union is strength," divided in the city, and there was but little hope that either faction would elect their ticket, Connolly managed to get a nomination for the State Senate; and by appealing to the national and religious prejudices of his country men, and by resorting to the "ballot stuffing and repeating," for which him and his confederates had become so notorious, he succeeded in having himself declared elected. According to Mayor Hall, whose knowledge of these matters can not be questioned, he made money out of his office—*not* out of his salary—but out of his *office*. Be this as it may, he was again set aside by his political friends, and remained in the background until 1868 when he was nominated for the position he now holds. For some time previous to the latter date, he had been employed as a clerk in the Central National Bank, at a salary of $2,500 a year. But as he had a couple of grown up daughters, who were the pride of his house and the light of his eyes, and who of course desired to be a credit to "Prappa," the anxious parent sometimes found it extremely difficult to keep up appearances, and make "both ends meet." This was his unenviable position when he was taken up by the Tammany leaders and placed in a position where his peculiar talents, and his utter lack of principle could be turned to the best possible advantage in promoting the schemes of his patrons. At this time John T. Hoffman was Mayor, and desired to become Governor. Peter B. Sweeny was City Chamberlain, and virtually controlled the finances of the city, so that Connolly was, in fact, only the nominal head of the Finance Department of the City Government. He was far too shrewd, however, to let other people indulge in wholesale robbery without having a share, the lions share, if might be, of the coveted spoils, and even if he had not been shrewd on entering the office, he received too many hints from the late James Watson, who held the position of County Auditor, not to fully realize the benefits to be derived from his office. Watson was a living and *active*, as well as *acting* illustration of what a man possessing an elastic conscience can do under favorable circumstances. He entered the Comptroller's Office a poor man, absolutely without a dollar, and had never received more than $7,500 a year, but at the time of his death, only four years after entering the office, Watson was worth between 2 and 3,000,000 of dollars. A famished tiger never rushed on its victim with more eager expectancy than Connolly rushed upon the people's money—but his expectations were disappointed. He found that unless he could adopt some expedient, the greater part of the money would be absorbed by those who had placed him in this position, while he would have to accept such crumbs of comfort as his masters chose to let fall from their table. A careful examination of the books and pay roll, developed the fact, important indeed to him, that the titles of several of accounts might be easily duplicated by using different phraseology to convey the same meaning, and that by making up pay rolls, and using fictitious names of persons "temporarily" employed in his department, he could even cheat the "heathen Chinee," who had invited him to take a hand in his little game of robbery. Hence, Mr. "Slippery," sat about finding additional titles for several of the accounts, and in this way "Adjusted claims," and "County Liabilities" became a part of the permanent debt of the city and county. Under the same skillful manipulation, County Contingencies, and "Contingencies in the Comptroller's Office," meant the same thing, as did also the amount charged in the city accounts, to make it less conspicuous. Again, there are three distinct pay rolls for the County Bureau. One of these contains the names of all the clerks regularly employed in the Bureau, and about a dozen names of persons who hold sinecure positions or—have no existence. The other two rolls contain about forty names, the owners of which, if indeed they ever had owners, have never worked one hour in the department. The last two are called "Temporary Rolls," and the persons whose names are on them are said to be "Temporary Clerks." Their salaries have become a part of the permanent debt of the County. There are numberless other methods, all of the same character, and all of which were but the different ways by which he filled his coffer at the expense of the people. How gross were the outrages, and how boldly they were executed, the public does not, even yet, fully know. In addition to the little arrangements we have mentioned, Connolly, like another illustrious benefactor of the "sovereign people," felt it incumbent upon himself, in consideration of the old adage that "charity begins at home," to see that his family, consisting of sons, son-in-laws, brothers, brothers-in-law, and cousins in every degree, were provided with fat offices and positions of trust—that is, where money enough would be entrusted to their keeping to make them comfortable for life.

In both cases, one at the expense of the nation, the other at the expense of a state, the plan worked well, and when neither the nation nor the state would submit longer, those who were deposed from office had become pecuniarily able to snap their fingers at the guardians of the people's rights. Connolly placed his son, who is a worthy representative of his illustrious sire, in the position of auditor in the city bureau, where all the claims for street paving, grading, and opening, &c., are paid, as are also the host of men who are borne on the rolls of the department of public works, the department of public parks, the fire and police department, and all the other departments of the city government, and where the opportunities for stealing were innumerable, of which he has not been slow to avail himself. His two sons-in-law he also placed in important positions, one as surrogate, the other as receiver of taxes. Not one of the three has either brains or energy enough to earn one hundred dollars a month at any legitimate business, if thrown on their own resources, but during the four years Connolly has been in office they have all amassed handsome fortunes. Tweed, Hall, Sweeny, and Connolly have been one in heart, soul, and purpose. Equally base, equally unworthy of trust or confidence, equally degraded and dishonest, they have been a most congenial quartette. Yet, with all their seeming unity, there was bitter hatred, suspicion, spying, and jealousy, cruel as the grave, between them. The great aim of the ring has been to surround themselves with men of their own stamp, and to concentrate all power in their own hands. Not one man can hold office under them who is not willing to sell his soul to them at the outset, and to embark in any scheme of villainy which will serve to prolong their term, or give them a continued lease of their present position, and who are not totally destitute of honesty and decency. John J. Bradley is state senator and city chamberlain. Thomas J. Creamer is state senator and tax commissioner, receiving for the latter office $10,000 a year. Michael Norton is state senator and one of the commissioners of the new court house. Henry Genet is state senator and a commissioner of the Harlem court house. Wm. M. Tweed is state senator and commissioner of public works. Frear, Speaker Hitchman, Dennis Burns, Thomas J. Campbell, Peter Mitchell, Richard

Flanigan, James Irving, and many other members of the assembly hold positions under city government. The several positions held by these men are either the gift of the mayor or the heads of the different departments, and when any measure affecting these functionaries comes up in the legislature, the entire delegation from this city have to vote ust as their master of the ring directs them. They are the machinery by which the rulers are enabled to perpetuate their power, but in addition to this, there is scarcely a keeper of a low groggery, policy dealer, a gambler, or a brothel keeper in the city whose name is not on the pay roll of he city government. If Connolly was an honest man, not one of these could receive a dollar from the city treasury.

PETER B. SWEENY.

The illustrious progenitor of this wonderful genius kept a rum shop on Park Row, and it was in this dingy abode, reeking with the fumes of whisky and the exhalations of the (literally) " unwashed Democracy," that Peter the *Small* first imbibed the knowledge of public affairs, and the lessons in state craft which have since made him so notorious. It is reported on good authority that Sweeny entered a law office while he was still a youth, and that it is to the smattering of the law which he then acquired that he owes his subsequent admission to the bar. Be this as it may, Sweeny never held any rank among the able lawyers of the New York bar. He found the problem of metropolitan politics much more easy of solution than the mastery of profound and knotty legal questions, and preferred to cultivate a more intimate acquaintance with the members of the "Spartan band" and the popular amusement of ballot-box stuffing, rather than to waste his time on the mere abstract philosophy of Kent or Blackstone. Acting on this principle, he sought and obtained the position of council to the corporation. This office required no legal depth or kuowledge, but an ingenious faculty for manipulating jobs, and as Sweeny was fully up to the required standard, and was even as utterly unprincipled aud utterly worthless as his urprincipled and worthless employers required him to be, he abundantly realized the expectations of the men who placed him in office, and was both useful and suecessful. At a more recent period, he was elected district attorney, but c onsious of his inability to bear a comparison with the eminent criminal lawyers who practice in our courts, he obtained leave of absence to go to Europe, and, on his return, resigned his position, and has since devoted himself entirely to politics. When Sweeny entered on the duties of city chamberlain, he astonished a good many simple-minded people by turning over the interest of the city deposits to the city treasury, where it properly belonged. But this very clever, and apparently disinterested act on the part of Mr. Sweeny, was only one of the many little tricks, transparent and shallow enough, to which he resorted, to throw dust into the eyes of the public; and while he was making a great parade of honesty in returning certain moneys to which he had not a shadow of a claim, he was conniving at a system of wholesale robbery, and participating in the profits accruing therefrom. Every fraudulent debt that was paid during his term in office was paid with his knowledge and consent, and, at least, tacit approval, as the checks that were paid out in liquidation of those were subsequently returned from the bank to Sweeny, as City Chamberlain, and were all recorded in the department of which he was head.

These checks bore on their faces proof of this fraud, and if Sweeny had been an honest man he would have exposed the treachery, and have thus saved millions of dollars to the taxpayers of the city. The private life of Mr. Sweeny has not been as entirely free from blemish as some of his most discreet friends could desire. In early life he was a "bunker" round an engine house, like his distinguished colleague, Tweed. I do not wish to be understood in thus referring to the early life of these men that it is a disgrace, or that they do not deserve great credit for the advance they have made. No nation in the world so glories in its "self-made men" as do the Americans. "Up from the depths"—"Out of the depths," have for us a meaning which none but we can understand. Still, we can but censure most keenly those who, having the power and the ambition to make of themselves something great, should waste that power by making themselves *only* great in the contempt of a nation. It is told of Mr. Sweeny, that being a bachelor at the time fortune began to shower her gifts upon him, he was not as mindful of the proprieties of life as he should be, though since many married men are not at all remarkable for the purity of their morals or manners, and he must have benefitted very much by the example of some of his married friends—Fisk, for instance, this is not to be wondered at. However, it is said that the lady who has the distinguished honor to be his wife, was for years his mistress, and that a little child was born—the living proof of shame and dishonor, and that it was not until the press began to talk of Mr. Sweeny for President of the United States, that he performed the tardy act of justice which legalized the relations between himself and the woman; and removed, in a measure, the stain that lay upon the brow of their innocent child. Think of this, oh voters of America! A man like him, devoid of even the first principles of honor and right and decency—a man whose name and record is a disgrace to the age in which he lives—a man whose crimes should have made him an inmate of Auburn State Prison long ago—*this man* to be elevated to such a position by your suffrage—*this man* to represent the people of the United States to all the world. Heaven help us, its no wonder Susan B. Anthony thinks you are making a muss of your politics, and that women had better take them in hand. In addition to those already enumerated, there are many other men whose antecedents will not bear examining, who hold high positions under the city government. Matthey T. Brenan, the sheriff, kept a groggery in the Sixth Ward, in his less prosperous days, than which none could be more vile. He is now one of the leaders of the Democracy, while his brother Owen is a prominent Tamanny Republican, and holds a couple or more profitable offices under the Ring, and another brother, who is a nondescript, holds a position in the Board of Education. But like Tweed and another American official before alluded to, it is not sufficient that the brothers of the sheriff should live off the taxpayers, but all the "family" must be provided for in the same manner.

"Mike" Malony and Wm. J. A. McGraph, the first a clerk in the Comptroller's Office, the last a clerk of Judge Dowling's, at the Tombs of the Police Court, are nephews of Brenan's. The earliest recollection of these fashionable young gentleman are of the misery, and filth, and squalor of one of the lowest rum stops on West street, where to use a filthy quotation, which does justice to their filthy characters, " they were mere grubs in the gutters of that wretched locality," but this was before, in the genial and exhilarating rays reflected from their great luminary of an uncle, they developed into butterfly exquisits, and were found to be at once useful and ornamental. John J. Bradly, brother-in-law to Peter B. Sweeny, first saw the light in a low groggory in Reade street, when it was considered one of the very worst streets in the city. During his early life he worked as hack driver, but had attained the dignity of livery stable keeper before he married the sister of Mr. Sweeny, and is now a millionaire. How long shall such men be permitted to rule New York, robbing them of their substance and disgracing our nation.

It seems almost useless to speak of A. O. Hall, the Mayor, a man in whom centers all that is villainous or corrupt—and who for a course of most unmitigated rascality can not be matched in the Old World or the New, and sickening as is the detail, and sickening as is the aggregate, it is yet necessary to speak of one whose career as a public man has been conspicuous for trickery and fraud while his private life is so revolting no pen can dwell upon its stained pages. It is marked by the grossest excesses, the most heartless betrayal of confidence and an utter disregard for the principles held sacred by all whose manhood marks them as separate and superior to brutes. As a politician he has "swung round the circle," having been by turns a Whig, a Know Nothing, a Republican, and a Democrat, at one time the most merciless enemy of our adopted citizens, and anon filling the role of a fawning sycophant, crouching at their feet to beg the office he could get no other way. Hall is charged by responsible parties with being a thief and the charge has been reiterated until it is familliar to every man, woman and child in America, and his feeble and futile efforts to free himself from the charge, were so weak as to be pitiable; and the flimsy tissue of falsehoods which he spread over it in his attempt to conceal it from the public, was so transparant as to even seem to magnify the first offense. He receives, as he deserves, in unlimited quantity, and unstrained quality, the scorn and contempt of those whom he has wronged and disgraced, as well as of the world at large. Confronted by his own guilt, we all know who were the dirty tools that he rallied for his defense. How "*ably*" that defense was conducted, and how in their eagerness to defend the man upon whom all their hopes in the future were centered, they bungled and stammered, and limped, and only succeeded in revealing more clearly than his foes had done, how deep and dark was the villainy he was engaged in. These things have been made too familiar to the people for it to be necessary for me to go into details, that would be wearying to you, but the time is past when men who have the power to adjust by their votes the affairs of city or state, will submit to such outrages.

The appointment of the committee of 70; to whose vigilance and untiring energy in bringing to light the dark deeds of the past four years, was a wise and prudent proceeding on the part of the people, and is having its desired effect. The Tammany Ring is broken—their stronghold is in ruins, never to rise again. Some of its members are in exile, and some in the hands of the law, and others the objects of a scrutiny from which they can not escape. It is well for the honor of our republican principles that justice should be dealt out to them in unsparing measure. It is well that the Christian influence which is so preeminent in America should forbid the longer continuance of a course of sin, to serve which everything that a people hold dear, everything for which the churches have labored, everything for which we have toiled and prayed, has been prostituted to their base ends. Now that their rule is broken, behold how shriveled and shrunken is their power—how like a thing of naught is their unholy ambition—how narrow the ledge on which they stand—only one word is needed, and that word has already gone forth, the fiat of an outraged and wronged people. Their ruin is as complete as their most relentless enemy could wish. We turn from the sickening and disgusting facts—we leave them alone in their defeat and disgrace, with the finger of scorn pointed at them by all the world—we look away into the future, and pray for bright days for the city and the state that have freed themselves from the yoke of their oppressors.

The Grave of COL. FISK, at Brattleboro.

FISK'S WILL.

Below is a true copy of Fisk's will as admitted to probate by Surrogate Hutchings.

The will was presented, the depositions of the subscribing witnesses and the oath of Mrs. Fisk as executrix being taken, all necessary conditions and preliminaries being complied with, the surrogate probate granting letters testamentary to Mrs. Fisk.

The estate was sworn to as not exceeding $1,000,000.

THE WILL.

I, James Fisk, Jr., of the city of New York, being of sound mind and memory, do make, publish, and declare this my last will and testament, hereby revoking all former wills by me made.

1. I give, devise, and bequeath all my estate and property, real and personal, except the special legacy hereinafter mentioned, to my beloved wife, Lucy D. Fisk, subject, however, to a trust to pay to my dear father and mother jointly, or to the survivor of them, $3,000 a year for their support during the life of them or either of them, and, further, to pay to Minnie F. Morse and Rosie C. Morse each $2,000 a year during their lives respectively until marriage, when the annuity of the one marrying shall cease. The property and estate aforesaid to vest absolutely in the said Lucy and her heirs forever, subject only as aforesaid; and the said trust shall not affect her right freely to dispose of and transfer any such property.

2. I give and bequeath to my sister, Mrs. Mary G. Hooker, stock in the Naragansett Steamship company of the par value of $100,000 for her sole and separate use forever.

3. I appoint my said wife and my friend Eben D. Jordan, of Boston, executors of this my last will and testament.

In witness whereof, I have hereunto set my hand and seal this 6th day of January, 1872.   JAMES FISK, JR.

SKETCH OF THE LIFE AND TRAVELS OF

Our Royal Guest,

THE GRAND DUKE ALEXIS, OF RUSSIA

CHAPTER I.

HIS RECEPTION IN NEW YORK—IN CHICAGO—INCIDENTS IN THE FAR WEST—HUNTING BUFFALO—CAMP SCENES—VISIT TO ST. LOUIS, MEMPHIS, NEW ORLEANS, ETC., ETC.

Believing that nothing could be more acceptable to my readers than a sketch of the life of our royal guest, the Grand Duke Alexis, of Russia, our relations to that mighty foreign power, both domestic and political, have long been of the most friendly and agreeable nature; indeed, America has been so prudent and cautious, and has so earnestly desired to promote the reign of "peace on earth, and good will to men," that there is but little cause for any nation to complain, and but little opportunity for any government to find "just cause or provocation" for ill-will. As has been justly remarked, there are many reasons why Russia and America should be more firmly allied than any other great powers. They are the two youngest empires on the face of the globe; for though our republic may be said to inherit the advantages and civilization of England, yet our government is even younger than that of Russia, and with everything in our favor, is making rapid strides towards that perfection which seems to

GRAND DUKE ALEXIS, of Russia.

belong only to maturity. Herein lies the difference. Russia is young in civilization, and also in power, while we advance in civilization under the experiment of a Republic. It is not strange, nor yet even selfish, that having seen our young nation rise from a germ upon which an oppressor had set his foot to crush out its life—to be one of the first powers in the world. That we feel a thrill of pride in her rise and prosperity, or that we ask with something of exultation if *this* is our youth, what will be our prime. Despite the apparent antagonism of our systems, and unrelenting despotism, and a freedom occasionally verging upon licence or lawlessness, there are no points of difference between this rigid European despot and the gigantic young American stripling, who, seeming to wear its republican principles and institutions so jauntily and lightly, yet guards them as the apple of its eye, and with a vigilance that neither sleeps or slumbers, and that never wearies. The two largest empires in the world, their paths are so distinct and different, as to render their clashing almost a moral and physical impossibility, certainly for ages to come, even if either party desired it, which they do not. A writer of more than usual philosophical research has said there is something remarkable in the peculiar geographical position of both the United States and Russia; for they both hang over the old and new world to pour their energy and life into the effete civilization of other empires. This may be fanciful, or only a pleasant conceit, but while Russia has whole provinces that are as yet almost unexplored, and is in a measure unconscious of its own power, and America is but a babe in years, taking its first firm steps alone, with the glory of the future, but just tinting with rosy splendor the young fresh face that is held up for the world's caress, we may indulge ourselves with the belief that these two powers who stand hand in hand at the beginning of the race, will in some way wield a mighty influence over the destiny of the world.

The visit of the son of the ruler of the youngest and most extensive empire existing, to the United States, is one of the most significant and interesting events of the year. It may mean much that is not seen upon the surface, or it may mean nothing. Long-headed politicians and shrewd diplomatists, however, look wise and smile blandly and complacently when they speak of it, and of the ready compliance of the Autocrat of all the Russians with the expressed wishes of our government with reference to the removal of the Russian minister. The purchase of Alaska from that power was looked upon as a most ridiculous thing, and every one wondered what use we could possibly make of a province that lay burried under a perpetual shroud of snow. It is yet quite likely that we have squandered millions to less purpose, and it will be strange if Yankee ingenuity will not find use for its many square miles. Be all this as it may, we do not attribute any immediate importance to the visit of the young Romanoff, but it is a pleasant extacy of courtesy between the two nations.

Nothing has been spared by our people to make his visit pleasant, and if the sober mind sometimes asks itself if it is strictly consistent with our democratic principles to lavish quite so extravagant a shower of attention upon a scion of nobility, when in this land of ' Spread Eagle " equality, every man is a soevreign, as a matter of taste, or a matter of policy, we can afford to let it pass. From New York to Chicago, and from Chicago to the Rocky Mountains, his course was one unbroken series of ovations. One thing which is told of him shows not only a kind heart, but a deal of delicacy and ingenuity in conceling his obligations to the people of the cities through which he passed. In New York he presented to the poor of that city the sum of $5,000, and many a heart that beat heavily beneath its weight of sorrow, and burden of poverty will bless his name. In Chicago a like sum was given, to be added to what has already been sent in from every quarter of the globe for those whom the merciless flames had stripped of their earthly all. The rivalry between the different cities through which he passed was of the most friendly nature, but the rivalry between the hotel proprietors was quite amusing. We give below a description of his reception by some of those important personages.

A FRIENDLY RIVALRY.

The arrival of the Grand Duke Alexis in this country has created great rivalry among the leading hotel-keepers. There is a disposition to make an impression in the ducal mind by these Bonifaces that each one is individually the only man in America who "knows how to keep a hotel." This rivalry is partly commendable and partly a censurable one.

IT IS VERY PLEASING

to the friends of the house to know their favorite stopping-place is so grandly upholstered in a supposed princely style and manner, but to the masses it is considered the height of snobbery. In this respect, however, the people display their prejudice through ignorance. They forget

THE FATHER OF ALEXIS IS VERY WEALTHY,

almost as rich as J. Y Scammon, or Deacon Bross, or one of the indicted aldermen. When Alexis was bidding his pa and ma goodby, the "governor" said: "Go my son; object is no money; scatter the chink and leave others to think; don't leave any trunks along the route as security for your board; pay as you go, and go it while you're young." Still his imperial highness does not like all this glitter and glory which is intended for him by

ENTERPRISING HOTEL PROPRIETORS.

He would be better satisfied if they would confine themselves to less display, and less flunkeyism. Of course he wants everything new, and comfortably fine, but he don't seem to relish the thought that he is enjoying himself with borrowed finery.

THE CLARENDON HOTEL

of New York, was the only improvised palace that has been or will be assigned the Duke as a temporary residence. The gorgeousness of its apartments was simply princely. It was undoubtedly the most elegantly-furnished hostelry ever provided for the reception of a guest, patrician or plebian, in this country. Gentlemen who saw it and are able to judge of its splendor, say

IT WAS AN INPERIAL PALACE.

The front of the house had been freshly painted; beyond this there was no external evidence of ostentation. A correspondent of *The Times* furnishes the following interesting description of the Grand Duke's residence while in Gotham: "Ascending about ten steps you reach the front door, of polished black walnut, with nothing extraordinary to attract the attention more than will be found at the entrance of any respectable merchant's residence. The door opens into a sufficiently spacious hallway, which ascends an elaborate staircase. Turning immediately to the right, after entering the front door, we pass into the

THE IMPERIAL APARTMENTS

of the Grand Duke. They consist of the three rooms upon the first floor. The front room is the parlor or reception-room. The centre room, approached through folding doorways, is the dining room. Next, approached by doorways, heavily curtained and draped with the richest damask and lace is

THE GRAND DUKE'S SLEEPING-CHAMBER.

From the front to the rear of the building, embracing three rooms, the distance is about 70 feet. The width of the rooms is 18 feet.

THE GRAND DUKE'S BED

is a pure white mat of sheep's wool. Another is in front of his toilet-case, and a similar one in front of his bureau. A gorgeous rug, with finely-wrought figures, is spread before the fireplace. The chandelier is the same as in the other rooms. Over the Grand Duke's bed, upon the wall, is the coat of arms of the imperial family of Russia.

SNOBBISH PROCLIVITIES.

There is a good disposition on the part of some people, snobs and shoddy aristocrats, to buy up the furniture and linen used in the ducal departments. The proprietors of the Russell house, in Detroit, were offered $500 for the bedstead on which Alexis slumbered, and the chambermaid was bribed in almost untold amounts to let a fashionable dressmaker of that city have the sheets. She said she would cut them up into handkerchiefs and sell to the bon ton.

CHAPTER II.

THE DUCAL PARTY AT BUFFALO.

Monday evening, says a Buffalo journal, will be long remembered as that which witnessed the finest performance, all things considered, of the opera of "Martha," that has ever been given in Buffalo. Expectation was keyed to a high pitch because of the excellence of the artists who were to appear—Parepa, Mrs. Seguin, Campbell, Castle, Seguin, and Hall, names great and ever memorable—and perhaps still more because it had been well advertised that the Grand Duke would be present. The managers of the academy and of the opera company regretted that they were not earlier advised of the ducal intention, as in that case they could have made their arrangements for his reception more perfectly, but, as it was, they did the best their circumstances allowed. Mr. Stanfield went to work, and, with his customary good taste and happy way of doing things in his line, improvised from the private box to the left of the stage and the two benches to its left, a very respectable apartment for the abode of royalty. American flags were frequent in the adornment, and a Russian flag here and there, besides other appropriate conveniences, were so happily arranged that they ought to have satisfied, and apparently did satisfy the simple tastes of Alexis. Whether interest to see the Duke or the attraction of the opera caused it, the academy was packed from floor to ceiling before the curtain rose; indeed we have never seen a finer audience there assembled.

A PUNCTUAL PRINCE.

Alexis, like a gentleman upon whom others are more or less depending, and one of princely education, arrived at the academy, with his full *suite*, promptly at eight o'clock. He was met at the door by Carl Rosa, and escorted to the seats provided. His *entree* was rapidly heralded, in that inexplicable manner by which such matters become known, through the vast audience, and there was a very perceptible buzz to the remotest corner of the theatre.

THE IRREPRESSIBLE GALLERY GODS.

When the Grand Duke appeared in the private box, he was greeted with as loud a cheer as the proprieties of the place admitted, and one *gamin*—who had sneaked in under the eyes of the vigilant door tenders—was heard to express the popular wish in the exclamation, "Come out and show yourself!" Alexis did come out and show himself, rejecting the box and taking his seat on the foremost of the enclosed benches, but we imagine not so much in obedience to the voice of the *gamin* as because he saw at once what all *habitues* of the Academy of Music have long since learned, that the poorest location from which to witness a performance is the boxes.

DIVIDING THE HONORS.

And now, before we say one word about the opera proper, we shall exhaust the personal connection of Alexis with it. He fairly divided the attention of the audience; for when attention was not commanded to the stage it rested upon him. Alexis, we may say, was neither backward nor forward in giving his applause to the performance; he observed the just medium. The wonderful notes of Parepa often claimed the approval of his princely hands—not that we think him any the better judge of music because he is a prince—and the archness and pretty coquetry of Mrs. Seguin frequently occasioned a smile, bordering on a laugh, to spread over his high-toned, imperially educated, and therefore, properly restrained countenance.

A ROYAL TESTIMONIAL.

His enjoyment of the opera was substantially expressed. Parepa was interviewed by W. F. Nachin, counsellor of state, accompanying H. I. H., and presented with a beautiful gold bracelet, the workmanship *a la Russe*, bejewelled with 12 torquoises and 28 diamonds, as a memento of the pleasure Alexis had received upon first listening to her incomparable voice.

AN INTERESTING VISIT.

The Grand Duke had a visitor on Monday evening, who was doubtless welcome to his highness.

About 6 o'clock in the evening an old lady, accompanied by a middle-aged man, apparently her son, called at the Tremont house and desired to see the Grand Duke. Mr. Drake endeavored to ascertain who she was, but her English was so imperfect that he could not understand her.

A GERMAN GUEST

of the house happened to be in the office when the ancient dame called, and Mr. Drake turned her over to him. They spoke together for a few minutes. At the conclusion of the conversation, the German gentleman announced that the old lady claimed to have been the wet nurse of the Grand Duke; and desired to speak with him about his infancy and boyhood.

This was enough for a reporter. He led the old lady to a seat in the hall.

A FEW WHITE LIES

about his connection with the imperial party was sufficient to cause the old lady to believe that she was conversing with one who was intimately conversant with the ducal habits and empowered to pilot her or anybody else into the presence of the overgrown infant whom she used to dandle on her knee one-and-twenty years ago. The reporter found to his chagrin that the old lady's knowledge of the correct pronunciation of the king's English was exceedingly limited, but that she had acquired a slight smattering of the *patois* of all nations to make herself partially understandable.

It would be useless to give the conversation as it occurred, for it took full ten minutes for the reporter and the old lady to come to an understanding upon any given question. He discovered at the very commencement that she had not been the Grand Duke's nurse, either wet or dry. Her name, she said, was Catharine Bakovitz. She used to live in St. Petersburg, and left there about ten years ago.

WHEN THE GRAND DUKE WAS A LITTLE BOY,

she had frequently seen him on the streets and parades of the Russian capital. He had always been a favorite with the citizens of St. Petersburg, and wherever he traveled in Russia he left a good name behind him for benevolence. Being an old woman, with no prospect of ever again seeing her own conntry, she wanted to look upon some member of the Russian royal family before she died.

At this juncture, the old lady produced

AN ENORMOUS PASSPORT,

which she had to obtain before she could leave Russia to come to America. It was covered with state seals, and was signed by the emperor and some of the chief officers. Her own name was also written upon it.

The reporter secured this treasured document, and had it sent up to the Grand Duke, rightly believing that it would obtain an audience for her more readily than a card or a mere verbal announcement. The messenger handed it to Admiral Possiet. He read it over carefully, and handed it to the duke's secretary, who passed it to another of the suit. Everybody read it before it reached the Grand Duke.

Meanwhile, Hons. Grinnell and Clark were introduced to the great Russian, and the old lady had to wait below in the hall. An hour passed by, and no messenger from the floor above appeared to usher her into the presence of him whom she longed to see. Another hour, and still no standing-haired Russian servant came with invitation or passport. Another hour, and the old lady began to grumble.

SHE APPROACHED THE REPORTER

again, and wanted to know why the Grand Duke would not see her.

"Doubtless he will," said the reporter; "give the young man time."

"What does he come to this country for if he does not want his own people to see him?" cried the old lady.

The reporter gave it up, and spoke to the clerk about it. That dignitary dispatched a golden-hair bell-boy to the heights above to make inquiries. The youth returned with a Russian, and the old lady and her son were

ESCORTED UP STAIRS.

The interview between them and the Grand Duke lasted almost twenty minutes, and Mrs. Bakovitz came down smiling and contented.

It was then 10 o'clock, and Alexis slipped between the ducal sheets to dream of Milwaukee.

ALEXIS' OPINION OF CHICAGO.

Mayor Medill is highly pleased with the young man, says he is not demonstrative, but educated and talented, and well posted on every subject presented. In the trip through the burnt district he expressed his opinions freely. He said the fire was

MUCH GREATER THAN HE HAD SUPPOSED

from the accounts, but that the part unburnt was also much greater, as he had no idea the city covered so large an area. He was confident that Chicago is all right for the future. Moscow, without any railroads, was rebuilt in less than ten years. Chicago, with her extensive railways, would rise from the ashes inside of four, or he was no prophet.

The water-works were wonderful to him, and the tunnel under the lake for such a purpose unparalleled in any country he had ever seen before.

The hog-killing which Alexis witnessed the day previous was not a new sight. He had seen the same operation in Copenhagen, only it took a little longer, and was carried still further, the hogs coming out from the process in strings of sausage, pleasant indeed for a Russian to contemplate.

A LESSON FOR A YOUNG PRINCE.

The Grand Duke Alexis is in a fair way to learn many things during his visit to this country, surprising to one who has been brought up in a royal court, where station and preferment are the privileges of hereditary rank or the rewards of favoritism, rather than of ability and merit. He is traveling with his eyes open, and is receiving new and strange impressions which may lead hereafter to important practical results.

During his recent visit to Connecticut, while he was passing through the cartridge factory at Bridgeport, in company with the governor of the state, he noticed the intelligent and respectable appearance of the workmen, and inquired if they were what were called the common people. Governor Jewell replied that they were a fair specimen of the working classes in this country. " But do you mean to say that these get into official position?" he further asked. " Perhaps not any of these men," rejoined the governor, " but men of their class do; they are intelligent, can probably read and write, and most of them take and read the newspapers." " Do you know of any cases where such men have actually been elected to office?" again queried the curious Alexis. " Oh, certainly," the governor said, " I myself worked in a shop as a tanner till I was twenty years of age," and the announcement seemed to puzzle the Duke a good deal.

Here was the governor of a state, as well-dressed and as well-appearing as himself, who had actually worked in a shop, and this man was welcoming him in behalf of a hundred thousand voters; it was more of an enigma than the boy had ciphered on previously.

Governor Jewell is not the only man in high position whom he will meet. In nearly every state, and even at the capital of the nation, whose president was a tanner, and one vice president a typesetter, he will find men occupying the high places of power and influence, who have risen from the shop of the humble mechanic, and by improving their limited opportunities have displayed such abilities that their fellow-citizens were glad to elevate them to posts of distinction and responsibility.

Nothing could be pleasanter than the hearty good will which the Grand Duke expresses both in word and act for our American people and our dearly beloved American institutions. The zest, almost boyish, yet so honest, frank and manly with which he has entered into the wild hunting sports of the west, showing that keen enjoyment was not only human, but *humanizing*, has gone far to remove any prejudice which might exist in the mind of those who are skeptical as to the "divine right of kings;" and a few slight extracts from the lengthy and tiresome newspaper reports may be interesting, the more so as the desire of our Royal Guest to witness and participate in the excitement of a buffalo hunt on the boundless prairies of the west, had been well known from the hour when he landed in New York. We will not lead you through all his travels, but presume you ara somewhat familiar with them already, and only mention that the party left the railroad at North Platte Station.

After a dash of thirty miles on horseback over the Western prairie, His Imperial Highness, the Grand Duke Alexis, and the whole distinguished hunting party have returned to camp, bringing their trophies and their honors with them. The Grand Duke has shown himself to be a thorough and successful sportsman. His noble bearing, his splendid horsemanship, and his battle with the buffalo of the first day's hunt have won for him the unbounded admiration of every member of the select and gallant company who witnessed them. His Imperial Highness has been looking forward to this occasion with special interest, and his anticipations have thus far been fully realized.

A SPLENDID SCENE.

More sport, however, awaits him. To-morrow is to be the grand chase, in which all are impatient to participate; and the Grand Duke and Sheridan and Custar in full gallop at the head, followed by the

THE GRAND DUKE ALEXIS.

other guests who compose this imperial hunting party, as well as by Spotted Tail, Pawnee Killer, Red Leaf, Whistler and other less celebrated chiefs, with their bands of ambitious Indian bevies, will constitute a scene such as never has been witnessed in these broad unbroken prairies.

ALEXIS KILLS THE FIRST HORNED MONSTER.

But already the ambition of the imperial sportsman has been partially gratified; and the special carrier, who carries this despatch to the nearest telegraph station, also bears a cable telegram from Alexis to his father, the Emperor, in St. Petersburg, announcing that he had killed the first wild horned monster that met his eye on the plains of North America.

THE FIRST HERD OF BUFFALO.

Very early in the morning Buffalo Bill went out to see what the prospects were. Before ten o'clock he returned with tidings that about fifteen miles distant there was a herd of buffalo browsing on the grass that grows on the divide between the Red Willow and the Medicine. This was pleasing news to the Grand Duke and all the other sportsmen. Orders were given at once to make the necessary preparations to follow and to find them.

TO HORSE! TO HORSE!

Accordingly, soon after breakfast, the hunters in our party, armed to the teeth, were snugly in their saddles. General Sheridan, being slightly indisposed, did not come out with us this morning, but we found in Custar, who was assigned the duty of the initiation of His Imperial Highness into the mysteries of buffalo hunting, the most dashing cavalry officer in the service, next to General Sheridan.

THE DUKE IN HUNTING ATTIRE.

The Grand Duke's hunting dress was very appropriate and simple. It consisted of jacket and trowsers of heavy grey cloth, trimmed with green, the buttons bearing the Imperial Russian coat-of-arms; he wore his boots outside his trowsers; his cap was an Australian turban, with cloth top. He carried a Russian hunting knife, and the Smith and Wesson revolver, recently presented to him, and bearing the coat-of-arms of the United States and Russia on the handle.

GENERAL CUSTAR'S APPEARANCE.

General Custar appeared in his well-known frontier buckskin hunting costume, and if, instead of the comical sealskin hat he wore, he had only had feathers fastened to his flowing hair, he would have passed at a distance for a great Indian Chief. Buffalo Bill's dress was something similar to Custar's.

When the three started off from camp together, the Duke, Custar and Bill—all large and powerful, and all hardy hunters—they attracted the attention and admiration of every one. Most of the members of the imperial party went along, and all the staff officers in camp.

THE FIRST CHARGE—ALEXIS BRINGS DOWN HIS BULL.

The Duke and Custar charged together, but what seemed singular to the hunters the buffalo did not run; they stood at bay, as if they had been expecting the imperial party, and as if to say "Come on," but Custar charged through an open space and scattered them. He kept his eye close on a big bull that was waiting "to go for" the Grand Duke. Alexis, however, rode close up to the animal and put a couple of pistol shots in him, when he started down the plane the Duke and Custar after him. Another pop from the pistol and he fell, when a shot from a rifle finished him.

THREE CHEERS FOR THE RUSSIAN HUNTSMAN.

A cheer arose from the company. When the Duke had got his game, out came his hunting knife and off went the tail of the dead buffalo, which he brought into camp as a trophy. Meanwhile the remainder of the few that were near enough were "gone for" by the other members of the party, and four buffalo were killed in all. One of them led

GENERAL SWEETZER AND MR. THOMPSON

a distance of three miles, but they finally brought him down. Count Olzonfieff secured his in gallant style, though the victory over the animal was not easily won. He who killed the other shall be nameless, but it is one of the incidents of the day that he secured his game.

A REMINISCENCE OF RUSSIA.

Two years ago to a day the Grand Duke was hunting with his father, and killed his first Russian bear. It delighted His Imperial Highness immensely to mention the incident that he killed his first buffalo on the anniversary of that day.

"Another bond of union between Russia and America," said a member of the Imperial party, while all joined in congratulations to the Duke.

THE GENTLEMEN FORMING THE IMPERIAL HUNTING PARTY.

The party consisted of his Imperial Highness the Grand Duke Alexis, His Excellency Vice Admiral Possiet, His Excellency W. F. Machin, High Councilor of State ; Count Olzenfieff, Mr. Bodisco, Consul General of Russia to the United States; Dr. Coudrin and Lieutenants Tudre and Startlegoff, of the Imperial Navy. These are the Russians, and they are accompanied by Mr. Frank Thompson, who manages all their railroad transportation and telegraphic business. The American gentlemen are Lieutenant General Philip H. Sheridan, General E. Ord, General Palmer, General G. A. Custar, General Sweetzer, and General Forsyth, Colonel Forsyth, Colonel Sheridan, and Dr. Asch, of the Lientenant General's staff, together with the *Herald's* correspondent. The officers of the cavalry companies present were Captain Egan, and Lieutenants Fowler and Allison, of Company K, and Lieutenants Stevens and Thomas, of Company E. Lieutenant Hays, of the Fifth Cavalry, attended to all the Quartermaster business in camp, and Lieutenant Clark accompanied General Palmer.

THE BANQUET ON THE WESTERN WILDS.

The dining-room of our camp is formed out of two large marquees, and is very handsomely festooned inside with flags. A sumptuous banquet was presented before the guests, after all had reached the ground last evening. The meal included different varieties of game to be found on the Western prairies. Choice wines were served with different courses. On the run to the Red Willow, Custar killed a prairie chicken with a rifle ball, and the Grand Duke was so delighted at the shot—it took off the chicken's head—that he wanted a slice of it for his dinner. Accordingly the bird was cooked after we came into camp, and the Duke relished it accordingly.

SINGING SONGS AND SPINNING YARNS.

After dinner some songs were sung and yarns were spun over the blazing camp fire, and, one by one, the members of the party retired to their tents to sleep, perchance to dream, of the expected buffalo hunt on the morrow.

At the risk of crossing the very narrow step supposed to lie between the sublime and the ridiculous, I must give you the account of this part of the affair, as furnished by the conscientious and no doubt truthful reporter of the *Post*. If any of my readers should suspect him of having drawn somewhat upon his imagination, I leave them to reconcile the matter as best they can, or will refer them to him for satisfaction.

The duties of hospitality required Sheridan to sing first, but he insisted that he was tired, had a cold, etc. However, after a good deal of urging, he pitched the tune with a dining fork, and sang to the air of "Johnny comes Marching Home," some *impromptu* verses of great excellence, the chorus, in which all joined uproariously, was

"And we'll all feel bad when
Aleck goes traveling home."

The Grand Duke then loosened his cravat, and sang the great national hymn of Russia, as follows, to a jerky gallopy tune which I cannot reproduce:

"Yanki dudelcom Tutown,
'Pon a littel poni,
Stucka fetherin Hiscap
Ancald itmac Aroni.

"Yanki doodel boishurra!
Downupside throthe middell
Yanki dudel fasolla
Withrum petdrum anfiddell."

This was greeted with wild applause, and when it had subsided, the company turned in anxious expectancy to me. I saw that they looked for something great. The Indians crowded around. After a few apologies about my throat, etc., I quietly opened that cartilaginous cavity, the larynx, and caroled the following affecting tale, to the air of that popular melody, Coronation:

"Five years ago—or—six—or so,
Pursued by wild hurrahs,
There came a runnin' down the street
Four persecuted squaws.

"Some wicked boys, with yells and noise,
Had, heedless of the laws,
With oyster cans and old tin pans,
Got after them four squaws.

"They wasn't dressed in fine array
Of hoops, and silk, and gauze;
Each wore a simple caliker skirt—
Them unprotected squaws.

"Right up my office stairs they hopped,
And screamed and put their paws
Upon my books, for they were scared—
Them four imperiled squaws.

"They never interfered with work,
They lectured for no cause;
They didn't ask the right to vote—
Them harmless, innocent squaws.

THE GRAND DUKE ALEXIS.   161

" Says I. ' Jim, take your shooting stick,
  And save them from the jaws
Of injury,' says I to him—
  ' These four fugacious squaws.'

" I opened up a law-book then,
  And pointed out the clause.
Says I, ' this ere will save those air—
  Those palpitating squaws.'

" Up spoke that valiant printer man,
  And boldly came to taw.
Says he to the boys, ' You'll shed sum blood
  Before you tech a squaw !'

" Lo ! vict'ry dawns ; the battle ends ;
  The dastard foe withdraws ;
We saved them for their anxious friends—
  Them four bombarded squaws !"

This was greeted with frantic cheers and some emotion. Sheridan bowed his head on my shoulder and wept quietly. Speckled Tail came and hustled me in a friendly manner, and said he owed me a debt of gratitude. Aleck held his hat before his face and hid his feelings. There are moments when we long to be alone.

At St. Louis, as elsewhere, Alexis received the most distinguished attention; and before his departure he was made the recipient of an appropriate memorial of his visit to this metropolis of a great mineral State, whose metallic wealth is yet in the first stage of development, but whose possibilities, under the quickening touch of capital and energy, are so magnificently promising. It was in the shape of a rosewood, plush-lined case, containing thirteen specimens of highly-finished Missouri iron, prepared by the Laclede Iron Mills, of this city. In addition, there was a volume, bound in Turkey morocco, formed of 480 sheets of *rolled iron*, each about the thickness of tissue paper, the whole being only one inch in thickness. These specimens shone like polished silver. The Prince, accepting this appropriate and graceful gift, promised to place it on exhibition at the Imperial Fair to be held in Warsaw in May next.

Back from the wild west with its exciting sports, back from the boundless savannas and rolling prairies, back from the rude people whose uncouth degredation makes us wonder whether they were included when it was written that " He formed man in his own image"—or wonder still farther if Darwin can by any possibility be right, and if so, whether—pshaw! I forgot that I was telling you of Alexis. I beg his Royal Highness' pardon and yours.

THE GRAND DUKE AT MEMPHIS.

The ball and banquet given to Alexis at the Overton Hotel, on February 3, was a grand affair, although the attendance was not large. Owing to the well-known aversion of the Duke to speeches, the formal reception, as originally laid down in the programme, was omitted. Dancing commenced at eleven o'clock and continued till 3. The ball-room was handsomely festooned with Russian and American flags. Over the main door was inscribed: "Russia and America," while above the main chandelier was a circle of gas jets forming the words, "Welcome Alexis." The royal party seemed to enjoy themselves exceedingly. After the ball they returned to their quarters at the Peabody Hotel.

The reception of the young Duke at New Orleans was worthy of the royal name she bears—worthy the far-spread fame of the "City by the Sea," and worthy of the guest to whom they did honor. We only wish it were in our power to give the details of his visit there, but to say that New Orleans was, as usual, master of the situation, is to say all we can for her; and we are sure that while he remembers the New World he will not forget the queen of the sunny South—decked like a bride in her orange blossoms, nor the courtesy and chivalry which has so long distinguished the Southern people, and which characterized his reception there.

Still on his triumphal march, still the object of admiration and attention, we can but hope that in the future only pleasant recollections of the "Land of the Free," may linger in his mind, and that in the years to come, mid the burdens and cares of state, or if dark days gather round him, or clouds hang threateningly above him, or danger and peril lie like pitfalls in his path, he may look back to those days with a thrill of affection for our country, and if more terrible times ever come when in the land of his birth he has not where to lie his head, then in the bosom of that glorious continent, where is found a refuge for the oppressed of all nations, and under the shelter of that flag, whose blue ground is brighter than the summer's sky, and whose stars rival those of a winter midnight, he will find a welcome and a home. Our best wishes will be with him where ever he may be, and may the two nations go on in peace and prosperity together.

ACCURATE, RELIABLE AND COMPLETE.

THE BOOK FOR THE TIMES.

THE YEAR OF BATTLES.
A HISTORY OF THE GREAT WAR
Between France and Germany:

Its, Origin, Causes, History, Biographies of its Leaders, Condition and Preparation of the Two Countries, Battles and Results.

BY L. P. BROCKETT, M. D.,

Author of HISTORY OF THE CIVIL WAR IN AMERICA; CAMP, BATTLE-FIELD AND HOSPITAL; WOMAN'S WORK IN THE CIVIL WAR, etc., etc.

WITH ABOUT ONE HUNDRED AND FIFTY MAPS AND ILLUSTRATIONS.

EMBRACING ALSO A COMPLETE HISTORY OF

Paris under the Commune, or the Red Rebellion of 1871

A SECOND REIGN OF TERROR, MURDER AND MADNESS.

This Work has been prepared with great care by an experienced and skilful writer on War topics, and its statements, drawn from offical or other perfectly authentic sources, will be found perfectly accurate and trustworthy. The descriptions of Battles are not mere sensational narratives, but while intensely interesting, are the work of a man who has gone step by step over the movements of the various Army Corps and Divisions in each battle, and comprehended the significance of each. It is no idle boast to say that the History is more accurate than could have been prepared in any other country, and that it has nothing to fear from any American competition.

It is Accurate, Reliable, and Complete.

On account of the immense sale which this Book is having, we have spared no money to make its mechanical execution complete and perfect in every regard. Where PLANS OF BATTLES have been found necessary to a proper understanding of the text, they have been given. That the WHOLE FIELD OF OPERATIONS may be taken in at a glance, we have put into the book an accurate and finely executed MAP OF WESTERN EUROPE.

THE NEEDLE-GUN, which has formed an important feature of the War, is shown by a diagram of twenty parts.

THE GREAT BATTLES OF THE WAR

are illustrated by Engravings designed by the artist who witnessed the terrible scenes of blood and carnage. The Work has been written in the author's finest style, and will be found equal to any of the popular books heretofore given to the world by him.

TERMS:

The work contains nearly 650 pages octavo, on good paper, and is illustrated by about one hundred and fifty excellent Maps, Diagrams, Battle Scenes, incidents and finely executed Portraits of all the Prominent Leaders on both sides. The book is published in English and German at the same price. The prices are:

Octavo, Cloth, Gilt Title, White Edges, - - $2.50.
" Leather, Gilt Title, Marbled Edges - - $3.00.

There is no better book for agents than this. Terms to agents are very liberal. Sample copy and outfit sent post-paid for $3, or a prospectus book for $1.25.

Address, as per title-page, to whichever is nearest.

HISTORY OF
THE GREAT FIRES
IN
CHICAGO AND THE WEST.

A Proud Career arrested by Sudden and Awful Calamity.—Towns and Cities Destroyed by the Devastating Element—Farms and Homes laid Waste—Scenes and Incidents—Losses and Suffering—Benevolence of the Nations, etc., etc.

With a History of the Rise and Progress of Chicago,
"The Young Giant,"
TO WHICH IS APPENDED
A RECORD OF THE GREAT FIRES OF THE PAST.

BY REV. E. J. GOODSPEED, D., OF CHICAGO.

☞ Illustrated with Large Engravings from Photographs taken on the Spot. ☜

The Profits on the Book will be devoted to the Relief of the Sufferers by the Fire.

CONDITIONS:

The work will contain about 700 crown octavo pages; will be printed on beautifully tinted paper, and will be illustrated by 75 superb engravings, some of them being nine inches square. Will also contain a large and accurate map, showing the whole city in wards, as well as the portion actually burned.

It will be well bound, in styles and at prices as follows:

English Cloth, Gilt Back, - - - - - $2.50
Arabesque Leather, Gilt Title, Marbled Edges, - - 3.00

The work will be sold only through our agents, and we agree that all who order the book will be perfectly satisfied, and at the same time will have the satisfaction of knowing that they have done something in the great work of relief.

This is the most Rapid Selling Book in America.

Printed in Dunstable, United Kingdom